TONI MORRISON

Recent Titles in Greenwood Biographies

TONI MORRISON

A Biography

Stephanie Li

GREENWOOD BIOGRAPHIES

GREENWOOD PRESS
An Imprint of ABC-CLIO, LLC

A B C 🟊 C L I O

Santa Barbara, California • Denver, Colorado • Oxford, England

Library of Congress Cataloging-in-Publication Data

Li, Stephanie, 1977-
  Toni Morrison : a biography / Stephanie Li.
    p. cm. — (Greenwood biographies)
  Includes bibliographical references and index.
  ISBN 978-0-313-37839-3 (alk. paper) — ISBN 978-0-313-37840-9 (ebook)
  1. Morrison, Toni. 2. Novelists, American—20th century—Biography. 3. African
American novelists—Biography. 4. African Americans in literature. I. Title.
  PS3563.O8749Z753 2010
  813'.54—dc22
  [B]   2009045233

14 13 12 11 10   1 2 3 4 5

This book is also available on the World Wide Web as an eBook.

Visit www.abc-clio.com for details.

ABC-CLIO, LLC
130 Cremona Drive, P.O. Box 1911
Santa Barbara, California 93116-1911

This book is printed on acid-free paper ∞

Manufactured in the United States of America

This book is dedicated to all the students who have read Toni Morrison's work with me. Our discussions have helped me understand her work in new and ever richer ways; in the classroom we fulfill her promise, "Look. How lovely it is, this thing we have done—together."

CONTENTS

Photo essay follows page 60

SERIES FOREWORD

In response to high school and public library needs, Greenwood developed this distinguished series of full-length biographies specifically for student use. Prepared by field experts and professionals, these engaging biographies are tailored for high school students who need challenging yet accessible biographies. Ideal for secondary school assignments, the length, format, and subject areas are designed to meet educators' requirements and students' interests.

Greenwood offers an extensive selection of biographies spanning all curriculum-related subject areas including social studies, the sciences, literature and the arts, history and politics, as well as popular culture, covering public figures and famous personalities from all time periods and backgrounds, both historic and contemporary, who have made an impact on American and/or world culture. Greenwood biographies were chosen based on comprehensive feedback from librarians and educators. Consideration was given to both curriculum relevance and inherent interest. The result is an intriguing mix of the well known and the unexpected, the saints and sinners from long-ago history and contemporary pop culture. Readers will find a wide array of subject choices from fascinating crime figures like Al Capone to inspiring pioneers like Margaret Mead, from the greatest minds of our time like Stephen Hawking to the most amazing success stories of our day like J. K. Rowling.

While the emphasis is on fact, not glorification, the books are meant to be fun to read. Each volume provides in-depth information about the subject's life from birth through childhood, the teen years, and adulthood. A thorough account relates family background and education, traces personal and professional influences, and explores struggles, accomplishments, and contributions. A timeline highlights the most significant life events against a historical perspective. Bibliographies supplement the reference value of each volume.

INTRODUCTION

Novelist, editor, scholar, teacher, public intellectual, mother, and contemporary griot for the African American community, Toni Morrison is one of the most influential writers in American history. Though nearing eighty years old, Morrison continues to produce eloquent, groundbreaking novels. Her wide-ranging additional pursuits—which have included decades of teaching, editing key African American texts, organizing collaborative artistic projects, and publicly commenting on important national issues—supplement a collection of novels that the Swedish Academy, which bestowed the Nobel Prize on Morrison in 1998, described as "characterized by visionary force and poetic import."[1] Despite her varied projects, Morrison insists that all of her work is united by a single concern. As she explains, "I know it seems like a lot, but I really only do one thing. I read books. I teach books. I write books. I think about books. It's one job."[2]

For Morrison, who began writing novels in her thirties, writing has become essential to her very existence. She has stated that "the only one thing that I couldn't live without is the writing."[3] This fundamental need to write highlights Morrison's deep commitment to the African American community as well as to the radical possibilities of narrative. She has explained that it is through story that we best understand others and hence recognize our role in and responsibilities to society. Stories nurture and enliven us, providing us with ways to make sense of both our world and ourselves.

Despite having published nine remarkable novels, Morrison continues her commitment to charting the contours of African American life through fiction. On days that she devotes to writing, Morrison gets up very early, often before dawn. In the dark, she makes coffee, drinking a cup as she watches the light come. Although this habit developed as a practical necessity when she was a single mother raising two boys and thus often needing to steal a few hours of her own, she later discovered that this practice complements her natural tendency to think best in the morning. She has observed that she is "not very bright or very witty or very inventive after the sun goes down."[4]

This ritual of watching the arrival of the light is crucial for Morrison to enter the state of mindfulness necessary for writing. Because she has penned most of her books while holding a nine-to-five job, Morrison has learned to work through and around interruptions. Continuous time for writing is a luxury she has rarely enjoyed. Consequently, she learned to adapt to the demands of her work and family life, perfecting a sentence or an image while washing dishes, preparing lunch for her children, or tending the garden. Morrison works her language carefully so that "the seams don't show." In fact, this labored process of revision is the secret joy of Morrison's writing process:

> I love that part; that's the best part, revision. I do it even after the books are bound! Thinking about it before you write it is delicious. Writing it all out for the first time is painful because so much of the writing isn't very good. I didn't know in the beginning that I could go back and make it better; so I minded very much writing badly. But now I don't mind at all because there's that wonderful time in the future when I will make it better, when I can see better what I should have said and how to change it.[5]

Morrison still starts to write by using yellow legal pads and sharp number two pencils. Because she does not actually like the act of writing, meaning the formation of letters, using pen and paper encourages her to be more economical in her writing; in order to limit tiresome handiwork she must capture an image or idea as succinctly as possible. Eventually, she transfers her work to a computer. Although she does not write every day, she thinks about her characters and their experiences constantly. She has stated that her fictional personalities become real for her at the point in which she falls in love with them. While she does not always agree with their choices, her love for them is absolute.

Though Morrison may not know where she will begin a novel, she always knows where it will end. Unlike many writers, she does not draw upon personal experience to write her books; as she explains, "I will use what I have seen and what I have known, but it's never about my life."[6] The imaginative process is key to her fiction, especially the way in which a single description can capture the complexities of human relationships. She frequently uses images to trigger an entire dramatic episode and to highlight essential qualities of certain characters; Pilate's lack of a navel illustrates her powerful will, Pecola's delight in drinking milk from a Shirley Temple doll reveals her desire to imbibe a new persona, and Sethe's black eyes suggest a woman who has seen far too much.

However, while images enliven and ground her writing, questions fundamentally drive her prose; she writes in order to understand certain dynamics or the nature of specific relationships—how does a child come to hate herself? What will a mother do to protect her child? How does a man achieve self-understanding? What is required to make paradise a livable reality? For Morrison, storytelling and the process of writing are ways to explore the central challenges of human existence—how individuals both flourish and hurt one another, how oppression operates, how communities sustain generations. Despite these myriad concerns, Morrison insists that her novels are unified by one central issue:

> All the time that I write, I'm writing about love or its absence. . . .
> About love and how to survive—not to make a living—but how
> to survive whole in a world where we are all of us, in some meas-
> ure, victims of something. Each one of us is in some way at some
> moment a victim and in no position to do a thing about it. Some
> child is always left unpicked up at some moment. In a world like
> that, how does one remain whole—is it just impossible to do that?[7]

Morrison's novels may be read as a sustained exploration of the nature of love, for it is love that motivates both her characters and her writing. In her work, love is never a simple matter of romance or familial commitment, but is instead composed of all the weaknesses and beauties of human need. Love can damage and heal, can nurture and destroy. Such too is the nature of Morrison's fiction; its power lies in language that moves readers to evaluate and even change their own lives. She has created a body of work that has inspired both sharp criticism and high praise, while also fundamentally transforming the American literary landscape.

Notes

1. "The Nobel Prize in Literature 1993, Toni Morrison," Swedish Academy (October 7, 1993).

2. Hilton Als, "Ghosts in the House: Profiles," *The New Yorker* (October 27, 2003): 66.

3. Robert Stepto, "Intimate Things in Place: A Conversation with Toni Morrison," in *Conversations with Toni Morrison*, ed. Danille Taylor-Guthrie (Jackson, MS: University Press of Mississippi, 1994), 23.

4. Elissa Schappell, "Toni Morrison: The Art of Fiction," in *Toni Morrison: Conversations*, ed. Carolyn C. Denard (Jackson, MS: University Press of Mississippi, 2008), 64.

5. Jane Bakerman, "The Seams Can't Show: An Interview with Toni Morrison," in *Conversations with Toni Morrison*, ed. Danille Taylor-Guthrie (Jackson, MS: University Press of Mississippi, 1994), 34.

6. Ibid., 39.

7. Ibid., 40.

TIMELINE: EVENTS IN THE LIFE OF TONI MORRISON

1931	Chloe Anthony Wofford is born on February 18 in Lorain, Ohio, to George and Ella Ramah Wofford.
1949	Morrison graduates from Lorain High School.
1953	Morrison receives a BA in English and a classics minor from Howard University.
1955	Morrison receives an MA in English from Cornell University.
1955–57	Morrison teaches at Texas Southern University.
1957	Morrison teaches at Howard University.
1958	Morrison marries Jamaican architect Harold Morrison.
1961	Son Harold Ford is born.
1964	Morrison is hired as senior editor with publisher L. W. Singer, a subsidiary of Random House, in Syracuse, New York.
1965	Son Slade Kevin is born. Morrison and her husband divorce.
1968	Morrison moves to New York City to work at the Random House headquarters.
1970	*The Bluest Eye* is published by Holt, Rinehart, Winston.
1973	*Sula* is published by Knopf.

1974   *Sula* is nominated for the American Book Award and receives the Ohioana Book Award. Morrison edits *The Black Book*, which is published by Random House.

1977   *Song of Solomon* is published by Knopf and is chosen as a Book-of-the-Month-Club selection.

1978   *Song of Solomon* receives the National Book Critics' Circle Award, the American Academy and Institute of Arts and Letters Award, the Oscar Micheaux Award, Friends of Writers Award, and the Cleveland Arts Prize for Literature. Morrison is named distinguished writer by the American Academy and Institute of Arts and Letters.

1980   Morrison is appointed to the National Council on the Arts.

1981   *Tar Baby* is published by Knopf. Morrison is elected to the American Academy and Institute of Arts and Letters. She appears on the cover of *Newsweek* magazine in March.

1983   "Recitatif," a short story, is published in *Confirmation: An Anthology of African American Women Writers*, edited by Amiri Baraka and Amina Baraka. Morrison resigns from Random House.

1984   Morrison is named Albert Schweitzer Professor of the Humanities at the College of the Humanities and Fine Arts at the State University of New York, Albany.

1986   Morrison writes *Dreaming Emmett*, an unpublished play that is performed at the Marketplace Capitol Repertory Theater of Albany under the direction of Gilbert Moses. It wins the New York State Governor's Award.

1987   *Beloved* is published by Knopf. It wins the Anisfield-Wolf Book Award in Race Relations.

1988   *Beloved* receives the Pulitzer Prize, the Melcher Book Award, the Robert F. Kennedy Book Award, and the Elmer Holmes Bobst Award for Fiction. Morrison is inducted into the American Academy and Institute of Arts and Letters and receives the City of New York Mayor's Award of Honor for Art and Culture as well as the Ohioana Career Medal Award. She also delivers the Robert C. Tanner Lecture at the University of Michigan. The title of her lecture is "Unspeakable Things Unspoken: The Afro-American Presence in American Literature."

1989   Morrison is appointed Robert Goheen Chair in the Council of the Humanities at Princeton University and receives the Modern Language Association of American Commonwealth Award in Literature.

1992   *Playing in the Dark: Essays on Whiteness and the Literary Imagination* is published by Harvard University Press. Jazz is published by Knopf. Morrison edits *Race-ing Justice, En-Gendering Power: Essays on Anita Hill, Clarence Thomas, and the Construction of Social Reality*, which is published by Pantheon.

1993   Morrison is awarded the Nobel Prize for Literature and in Paris the Commander of the Order of Arts and Letters. She writes lyrics for "Honey and Rue," a cycle of six songs commissioned by Carnegie Hall for soprano Kathleen Battle, with composer Andre Previn. She founds the Princeton Atelier, a studio arts program that gathers students, faculty, and visiting artists to collaborate on visual art, literature, dance, film, theater, and music.

1994   Morrison receives the Premio Inernazionale "Citta dello Stretto," the Rhegium Julii in Reggio Calabria, Italy, and the Condorcet Medal. She writes lyrics for "Four Songs" with composer Andre Previn. "Four Songs" is performed by Sylvia McNair at Carnegie Hall.

1996   Morrison is named Jefferson Lecturer in the Humanities by the National Endowment for the Humanities. She is awarded the National Book Foundation Medal for Distinguished Contribution to American

Letters. *The Dancing Mind*, a National Book Foundation Lecture, is published by Knopf. Morrison makes her first appearance on Oprah's Book Club with *Song of Solomon*.

1997   With Claudia Brodsky Lacour, Morrison edits *Birth of a Nation'hood: Gaze, Script and Spectacle in the O.J. Simpson Case*, which is published by Pantheon. She writes lyrics for "Sweet Talk" with composer Richard Danielpour. "Sweet Talk" is performed by Jessye Norman at Carnegie Hall.

1998   *Paradise* is published by Knopf. With composer Richard Danielpour, Morrison writes lyrics for "Spirits in the Well," which is performed by Jessye Norman at Avery Fisher Hall. She receives the Medal of Honor for Literature by the National Arts Club in New York and is named A.D. White Professor-at-Large at Cornell University. The movie *Beloved*, directed by Jonathan Demme and starring Oprah Winfrey, premieres. Morrison receives a Grammy nomination for Best Spoken Word Album for *Beloved*. In an article in the *New Yorker*, Morrison calls President Bill Clinton "our first black President." She also edits the collected essays of James Baldwin for the Library of America Series.

1999   *Paradise* receives the Ohioana Book Award for Fiction and the Oklahoma Book Award. Morrison is named *Ladies Home Journal* Woman of the Year. *The Big Box*, a children's book she coauthors with son Slade Morrison, is published by Hyperion.

2000   Morrison writes lyrics for *Woman.Mind.Song*, composed by Judith Wier and performed by Jessye Norman at Carnegie Hall. She is awarded the National Humanities Medal.

2001   Morrison receives the Pell Award for Lifetime Achievement in the Arts, the Jean Kennedy Smith NYU Creative Writing Award, and the Enoch Pratt

Library Lifetime Achievement Award. She is also awarded the Cavore Prize in Turin, Italy.

2002　With composer Richard Danielpour, Morrison writes the libretto for *Margaret Garner*, which is co-commissioned by the Michigan Opera Theatre, the Cincinnati Opera, and the Opera Company of Philadelphia. *The Book of Mean People*, a children's book coauthored with Slade Morrison, is published by Hyperion. *Five Poems*, illustrated by Kara Walker, is published in limited edition by Rainmaker Editions of Las Vegas, Nevada.

2003　*Love* is published by Knopf. Two children's books in the *Who's Got Game?* series, a collaboration with Slade Morrison, are published by Scribner's: *The Ant or the Grasshopper?* and *The Lion or the Mouse?* Morrison receives Docteures Honoris Causa from the Ecole Normale Superieure in Paris, France.

2004　*Remember: The Journey to School Integration*, a history book for children, is published by Houghton Mifflin. Morrison receives the Academy of Culture "Arts and Communities" Award in Paris, France, and delivers the Amnesty International Lecture in Edinburgh, Scotland. She also receives the NAACP Image Award for Outstanding Literary Work, Fiction. Coauthored with Slade Morrison, *Who's Got Game Series: Poppy or the Snake?* is published by Scribner's.

2005　Morrison receives the Coretta Scott King Award from the American Library Association. *Margaret Garner* premieres at the Michigan Opera Theatre in Detroit. Coauthored with Slade Morrison, *Who's Got Game Series: The Mirror or the Glass?* is published by Scribner's.

2006　*Beloved* is chosen as the Best Work of American Fiction of the Last 25 Years by the *New York Times*. After seventeen years, Morrison retires from Princeton. A salute is held in her honor at Lincoln Center in New York. Morrison curates "A Foreigner's

Home," an exhibit at the Louvre Museum in Paris. *The Bluest Eye*, adapted for the stage by Lydia Diamond and directed by Hallie Gordon, premieres at the New Victory Theatre in New York.

2007   Morrison curates "Art Is Otherwise" Humanities Programs, sponsored by the French Alliance, in New York City.

2008   Morrison endorses Barack Obama for president of the United States in a widely published letter addressed to the Illinois senator. *A Mercy* is published by Knopf.

2009   Morrison edits *Burn This Book: PEN Writers Speak Out on the Power of the Word.*

Chapter 1

EARLY LIFE AND FAMILY

Toni Morrison was born Chloe Ardelia Wofford in Lorain, Ohio, a small, industrial town located twenty-five miles west of Cleveland and bordering Lake Erie. Lorain continues to be a town largely dependent upon the steel industry, and in 1931, the year of Morrison's birth, it was heavily populated with migrants from Europe, Mexico, and the American South. Morrison grew up among working families of all colors, families who struggled through the Great Depression and valued hard work and integrity. While many Americans lost confidence in banks and the economic system as a whole, following the fall of the stock market in 1929, Morrison was raised to trust her community, her family, and, most crucially, herself.

The second of four children, Morrison was born at home, at 2245 Elyria Avenue, one of a series of look-alike two-story homes that are within walking distance of the Black River, a small tributary that empties into Lake Erie. The Woffords lived in more than six different apartments throughout Morrison's childhood. On one occasion, when the family could not afford the four-dollar monthly rent, the landlord set their apartment on fire. The Woffords responded with laughter and moved to a new apartment.

Morrison's parents, George and Ella Ramah Wofford, were both from the South; George was born in Cartersville, Georgia, and Ramah in Greenville, Alabama. Despite this similarity, they had opposite views of the South. Although George considered Georgia to be the most racist state in the country and did not believe that such entrenched bigotry would ever change, he often went back to visit his family. Ramah, by contrast, remembered the South fondly but refused to ever return. These paradoxical attitudes strongly influenced Morrison, who grew up without a singular conception of the South as either wholly violent or as romantically idyllic. As she would later demonstrate in her fiction, exaggerated binary oppositions never capture the complexity of life. Instead, the truths of a place, like the motivations of an individual, are neither entirely good nor entirely bad but are born of fundamentally human desires and needs.

A hardworking shipyard welder, George worked at U.S. Steel, which prospered during World War II and employed a variety of newly transplanted immigrants from Poland, Greece, and Italy. Morrison's father held as many as three jobs at once and firmly believed in the moral superiority of African Americans. After welding a perfect seam, George put his initials on it, and though the young Morrison told her father that no one would see it, he replied, "But I'll know it's there."[1]

George's proud work ethic was coupled with a fierce suspicion of white people. Morrison has commented that she "grew up in a basically racist household with more than a child's share of contempt for white people."[2] She was raised to believe that white racism was derived from an intellectual or emotional deficiency and therefore its purveyors could only be pitied for their unfortunate weakness. In a 1976 essay for the *New York Times Magazine*, Morrison describes watching her father assault a white man who one day mysteriously appeared outside their apartment. George assumed that the man had come to molest his daughters, and though in hindsight Morrison thinks her "father was wrong . . . considering what I have seen since, it may have been very healthy for me to have witnessed that as my first black-white encounter."[3] As she later reflected, "Seeing that physical confrontation with a white man and knowing that my father could win thrilled, excited, and pleased me. It made me know that it was possible to win."[4] Despite his light skin, George favored darker-skinned blacks, a preference shared by Morrison's very black great-grandmother, who found impurity in those with whiter complexions.

Morrison's great-grandmother was part Native American and told stories from the time of slavery. Although she owned property in the Jim Crow South, having inherited eighty-eight acres of land from her parents, the family was fearful of local whites. Her five-year-old son, John Solomon Willis, hid under a bed when he heard that "the Emancipation Proclamation was coming"; the boy assumed that anything from whites was dangerous and thus best avoided. Morrison has described her grandfather as "an unreconstructed black pessimist" who was convinced that whites would always unite to defeat the progress of blacks.[5] This attitude derived from a long life of discrimination and injustice. As an adult, John Solomon lost the family's farm to land swindlers and was forced into sharecropping, a common labor arrangement in the South in which poor blacks worked the farm of a white landowner. Although theoretically they were to share the profits of the farm, most blacks fell into perpetual debt caused by the inflated cost of rent, seed, fertilizer, and other necessities. John Solomon was a skilled carpenter, but he struggled to find work since employers favored white immigrants and former convicts. Unable to provide for his wife, Ardelia, and their seven children, he left for Birmingham, where he worked as a jazz musician, and sent money to his family as often as he could.

By 1912, Ardelia could hardly keep up with the work of the farm and she became increasingly fearful that the family's landlord would seek revenge for John's departure. She thus resolved to join her husband in Birmingham. She secretly made travel arrangements for the family, and late one night, she led her children off the farm and to the train station. With only eighteen dollars, the family arrived not knowing whether John Solomon had received the message announcing her plans. Initially, no one was there to meet their train in Birmingham. They waited for an agonizing hour, unaware that John Solomon was watching them the entire time. He stayed hidden, afraid that someone might recognize and capture him for owing money. He revealed himself only when he was sure that there was no immediate danger to his family.

Despite their joyful reunion, life continued to be difficult for the Willis family in Birmingham. In the decades of the early twentieth century, Birmingham was a major center for the Ku Klux Klan and was extremely hostile to African Americans. After a few years, the family moved to the Cumberland Mountains of Kentucky, joining a general movement of African Americans to the North known as the Great Migration. This massive population shift of approximately seven million blacks from the South to the North was propelled by a general desire to escape racism, increased employment opportunities in the industrial cities, and the hope for a better education. All of these causes led Morrison's family to seek a more promising life in the North. Eventually, this fierce commitment and sense of hope propelled them even further from the South. Ardelia convinced her husband that they would have to leave Kentucky when she discovered that her children's schoolteacher did not know how to do long division. For Morrison's grandmother, progress for African Americans was "like the slow walk of certain species of trees from the flat-lands up into the mountains . . . the signs of irrevocable and permanent change."[6] It would take generations to create lasting shifts, but only two in the Willis family to move from sharecropper to Nobel Prize winner.

A dedicated member of the African Methodist Episcopal Church, Morrison's mother, Ramah, inherited Ardelia's hope for achieving racial harmony and instilled in her children values of self-reliance, community, and family. She expected her daughters to be strong and aggressive, like the elder women in the family, women who took on both work and family responsibilities without complaint. As an adult, Morrison came to realize that such behavior could be considered "feminist," but in her family it was simply the fulfillment of one's basic duties to others.

In contrast to her husband's firm distrust of white people, Morrison's mother "*believed* in them—their possibilities."[7] Ramah wrote a letter to President Roosevelt to complain about a bug-ridden meal the family received while on relief, and because the meals improved, she was convinced that Roosevelt had personally responded to her message. She routinely walked down to the local movie theater to make sure that the owners were not segregating blacks and whites. Ramah reasoned with bill collectors, believing that they needed only to be reminded of her absolute commitment to good credit; surely her word was enough cause to be given more time. Nonetheless, a degree of skepticism about white people abided, for as Morrison explains, "Both my parents believed that all succor and aid came from themselves and their neighborhood." The Woffords always relied first upon family rather than upon outsiders. Ultimately, Morrison would pass on to her own children a certain amount of suspicion about white people, noting, "I teach my children that there is a part of yourself that you keep from white people—always."[8]

As a capable and efficient homemaker, Ramah early on realized that her second child had talents beyond domestic chores. Morrison recalls once trying to hang up a pair of pants outside by pinning the inside pockets to the clothesline. Her efforts were met with the amusement of her mother and grandmother. While Morrison was not an ideal helpmate around the house, she participated vigorously in nightly gatherings that abounded with stories, music, and song. Ramah sang arias from *Carmen* and Ella Fitzgerald tunes while Morrison's grandfather often played the violin after dinner, encouraging everyone to dance. The young writer grew up listening to her parents spin long, enchanting tales of deceased relatives, ghosts, and powerful dreams. Her grandmother kept a book that translated dream images into a three-digit number that was used to play in various games. Certain dream images also connoted precise meanings; for example, a wedding signified death and vice versa.

As a child, Morrison also became attentive to the nuances of her family's language, which changed according to different circumstances. She explains, "In my family, when something terribly important was to be said, it was highly sermonic, highly formalized, biblical in a sense, and easily so. They could move easily into the language of the King James Bible and then back to standard English, and then segue into language that we would call street. It was seamless."[9] Morrison remembers that storytelling in her family was a collaborative effort, an activity shared by men and women as well as by people of all ages. In an interview with the *Lorain Journal*, Ramah described how her daughter asked for so many stories that "Finally I'd get tired of telling the stories over and over again. So I made up a new story."[10]

Morrison has two younger brothers, but while growing up she was closest to her sister, Lois, who is only a year and a half older. The two still talk by phone almost every day. Morrison recalls how family and friends used to call out for the two girls, "Loisandchloe! Where's Loisandchloe?" such that she "wasn't sure which part of that was my name."[11] The girls played with other neighborhood children, making dolls out of hollyhocks and toothpicks. However, their favorite activity involved storytelling and frequent trips to the town library. Though the Woffords changed apartments frequently, they were always close to the library. During high school, Morrison worked as the secretary to the head librarian in Lorain. When officials from Lorain suggested that a statue be erected in her honor or a street named after her, Morrison preferred to have her name attached to the Lorain Public Library; its reading room is now named the Toni Morrison Room.

Lorain was a city small enough to foster a close-knit community. Morrison remembers that even neighborhood men who were vaguely associated with criminal activity, like selling liquor and gambling, kept a steady eye out for her and her sister. Once as a teenager walking in Lorain, Morrison was stopped by a stranger who asked, "Are you a Willis?" referring to Ramah's maiden name. When Morrison replied in the affirmative, the man said, "I thought so. You walk like one."[12] In a 1979 interview, Morrison recalled that as a child she and her sister were often called upon to find her grandfather if he happened to wander off. She told this story to highlight how communities have changed; the husband of a family friend had recently suffered a heart attack while walking alone and had been discovered dead in a field months later. Morrison grew up in a world in which neighbors and even casual strangers looked after one another, creating a strong network of support. Most importantly, children understood themselves to have clear responsibilities to their elders; Morrison knew to read the Bible to her grandmother and to bring her grandfather walnuts, and she passed on this kind of respect to her sons. As she explains, the simple expectation that her young boys were to bring her mother her orange juice was "part of knowing who they are and where they came from. It enhances them in a particular way, and when they have children of their own it won't be this little nuclear you and me, babe."[13]

The strength of the African American community has been one of the most important themes in Morrison's novels. In *Sula*, the Bottom community acts like a Greek chorus to comment upon the actions of the main characters. The misguided materialism and individualism of *Song of Solomon*'s Macon Dead is highlighted by his estrangement from the black community and in particular from his wise sister, Pilate. However, while Morrison repeatedly emphasizes the need for strong social networks, her depiction of the African American community includes sharp critique. In *The Bluest Eye*, she faults Pecola Breedlove's community for championing ideals of physical beauty based upon whiteness and thus for contributing to the young girl's demise. The black communities in *Sula* and *Beloved* exile Sula and Sethe respectively as punishment for behavior they conceive to be too transgressive. Morrison acknowledges the nurturing aspects of the African American community without ignoring its faults. Instead, she recognizes its constructive and necessary place in black life as a key source of identity and cultural survival.

Morrison was the only child in her kindergarten class who could read, having been taught by her parents. In interviews she claims not to remember being in the world before becoming literate. Her first memory is of writing on cement sidewalks with Lois when she was about three years old. Morrison came to share Ramah's love of reading and recalls her mother's excitement upon receiving the latest book-club selection, that is, when the family could afford such luxuries. Morrison was especially fond of the works of Leo Tolstoy, Fyodor Dostoyevsky, Jane Austen, and Gustave Flaubert, noting: "Those books were not written for a little black girl in Lorain, Ohio, but they were so magnificently done that I got them anyway—they spoke directly to me out of their own specificity. I wasn't thinking of writing then . . . but when I wrote my first novel years later, I wanted to capture that same specificity about the nature and feeling of the culture I grew up in."[14] Morrison has consistently emphasized that universality exists in the particulars of a specific social and historical context. Moreover, just as Austen and Dostoyevsky did not simplistically explain their world to audiences unfamiliar with Victorian social customs or Russian religious beliefs, Morrison does not offer facile depictions of black life to a white audience. Instead, her novels demand rigorous engagement from all readers, requiring them to understand Morrison's world on its own terms.

Morrison had already read *The Adventures of Huckleberry Finn* (1884) when her junior high school class was assigned the classic American text. The "fear and alarm" that Morrison felt upon her first reading of the book was compounded by her English teacher's uncritical treatment of the text. As she explains in a 1996 introduction to Twain's novel:

> It provoked a feeling I can only describe now as muffled rage, as though appreciation of the work required my complicity in and sanction of something shaming. Yet the satisfactions were great: riveting episodes of flight, of cunning; the convincing commentary on adult behavior, watchful and insouciant; the authority of a child's voice in language cut for its renegade tongue and sharp intelligence.[15]

Morrison's early experience with *The Adventures of Huckleberry Finn* enacts a kind of readerly double consciousness, a term first used by noted African American scholar and writer W. E. B. Du Bois. He writes in his influential *The Souls of Black Folk* (1903):

> It is a peculiar sensation, this double-consciousness, this sense of always looking at one's self through the eyes of others, of measuring one's soul by the tape of a world that looks on in amused contempt and pity. One ever feels his two-ness,—an American, a Negro; two souls, two thoughts, two unreconciled strivings; two warring ideals in one dark body, whose dogged strength alone keeps it from being torn asunder.[16]

Morrison perceived the racism of *The Adventures of Huckleberry Finn* even as she was moved by its clever narrator and amusing episodes. As a literary critic, Morrison has done much to explore the ways in which white-authored texts exploit black stereotypes to create an idealized version of American identity. Her childhood encounter with *The Adventures of Huckleberry Finn* laid the groundwork for some of her most important theoretical insights.

When Morrison was twelve years old she began working after school, cleaning house for a rich white woman. As a young girl, she was impressed by the opulence of her employer's home, which had wall-to-wall carpeting and an automatic washing machine. She earned two dollars and fifty cents every Friday, half of which she proudly gave to her mother. Morrison derived immense pleasure from knowing that part of her wages paid for household expenses and hence were "used for real things: an insurance policy payment maybe or the milkman."[17] When the work became arduous, Morrison was aware that should she quit, her family would suffer the loss.

At one point, Morrison's employer offered her clothes but made clear that Morrison would have to pay for these used garments. With only two dresses of her own, Morrison happily bought the castoffs with her weekly wages. However, when Ramah asked her daughter if she wanted to work for used clothes, Morrison decided to return her employer's garments in exchange for her wages. This experience also taught Morrison that complaints about work would garner no sympathy from her father. He met his daughter's grumbles with a stern reminder: "Listen. You don't live there. You live here. At home, with your people. Just go to work; get your money and come on home."[18] Morrison was expected to do her work well and without complaint, just like her elders, and to return to a life fundamentally based in her family.

Notes

1. Hilton Als, "Ghosts in the House: Profiles," *The New Yorker* (October 27, 2003): 67.

2. Toni Morrison, "A Slow Walk of Trees (as Grandmother Would Say), Hopeless (as Grandfather Would Say)," in *What Moves at the Margin: Selected Nonfiction*, ed. Carolyn C. Denard (Jackson, MS: University Press of Mississippi, 2008), 7.

3. Ibid., 6.

4. Als, "Ghosts," 67.

5. Morrison, "A Slow Walk," 3.

6. Ibid., 5.

7. Ibid., 6.

8. Colette Dowling, "The Song of Toni Morrison," in *Conversations with Toni Morrison*, ed. Danille Taylor-Guthrie (Jackson, MS: University Press of Mississippi, 1994), 51.

9. Sheldon Hackney, "'I Come from People Who Sang All the Time': A Conversation with Toni Morrison," in *Toni Morrison: Conversations*, ed. Carolyn C. Denard (Jackson, MS: University Press of Mississippi, 2008), 131.

10.   Qtd. in Als, "Ghosts," 67.

11.   Adam Langer, "Star Power," in *Toni Morrison: Conversations*, ed. Carolyn C. Denard (Jackson, MS: University Press of Mississippi, 2008), 210.

12.   Hackney, "'I Come from People,'" 135.

13.   Charles Ruas, "Toni Morrison," in *Toni Morrison: Conversations*, ed. Carolyn C. Denard (Jackson, MS: University Press of Mississippi, 2008), 104.

14.   Jean Strouse, "Toni Morrison's Black Magic," *Newsweek* (March 30, 1981): 54.

15.   Toni Morrison, "[This Amazing, Troubling Book]," in *Adventures of Huckleberry Finn: An Authoritative Text, Contexts and Source Criticism*, 3rd ed., Mark Twain, ed. Thomas Cooley (New York: W.W. Norton & Company, 1999), 385.

16.   W. E. B. Du Bois, *The Souls of Black Folk* (New York: Dover Publications, 1903), 2.

17.   Toni Morrison, "She and Me," in *What Moves at the Margin: Selected Nonfiction*, ed. Carolyn C. Denard (Jackson, MS: University Press of Mississippi, 2008), 16.

18.   Ibid., 16.

Chapter 2

EDUCATION AND EARLY CAREER

In Lorain, Morrison attended integrated schools, where she consistently impressed her teachers. One of Morrison's junior high school instructors sent her home with a note that stated, "You and your husband would be remiss in your duties if you do not see to it that this child goes to college."[1] Although Lorain lacked the bigotry and overt discrimination of the South, Morrison was acutely aware of racial differences. When she was in the fifth grade, a new boy whose family had just moved to the United States arrived in her classroom. Morrison was often selected by her teacher to introduce new immigrant children to the routine and expectations of schoolwork. She helped teach the boy to read, but the moment that "he found out that I was black—a nigger," they became members of separate groups. As she explains, "That's the moment when he belonged, that was his entrance . . . He had to come above at least one group—and that was us."[2] This incident highlights one of the abiding insights of Morrison's literary and critical work—that historically American identity has been based on exclusion and requires a black other against which to define itself. Even children are subject to the pernicious effects of race as they adopt categories of difference that lead to discrimination and hatred.

At Lorain High School, Morrison was an active member of the debate team, the yearbook staff, and the drama club. Although only one member of her family had attended college, she was determined to continue her education at the university level after abandoning her dream to become a dancer like Maria Tallchief. Following her desire to be surrounded by black intellectuals, in 1949 she enrolled at Howard University, where she studied English literature and the classics. One of the premier all-black universities in the nation, Howard has a long history of academic excellence. There she studied under Alain Locke, a key figure of the Harlem Renaissance and editor of *The New Negro: An Interpretation* (1925), an influential anthology of African American writing.

George Wofford took a second union job so that he could afford his daughter's tuition at Howard though this broke the employment rules of U.S. Steel. When his supervisors discovered his breach of contract, George replied that if they fired him, he would only find another job in order to finance the education of his two daughters; Lois had begun college a few years earlier. George was allowed to keep both jobs. Ramah also started working so that she could send her youngest daughter pocket money. She handed out towels at an amusement park restroom. Along with her tips, she sent Morrison packages of crackers, canned tuna, and sardines.

While in college, Morrison changed her name to Toni, a reference to Anthony, the baptismal name she received after converting to Catholicism when she was twelve. Poet and leader of the Black Arts Movement Amiri Baraka was two years behind Morrison at Howard and remembers her as "one of the most beautiful women I'd ever seen."[3] Though the two would eventually collaborate on artistic projects, during college Baraka was too shy to approach her. Morrison thrived intellectually at Howard, but she was taken aback by the segregated buses of Washington DC as well as by the informal color hierarchy enforced by the students. According to the "paper bag test," students were divided by skin color into social groups in which a lighter complexion signified privilege and desirability. She recalls once telling a classmate at Howard that she had a friend who studied at the Goodman Theatre. Her companion was surprised because she knew of no black students there. Morrison's classmate could not fathom the truth, which was that the friend Morrison had mentioned was not black.

Morrison joined the theatrical group, the Howard University Players, where she encountered students who were more concerned with talent than with color. The troupe performed throughout the South and occasionally would stay with members of the local Zion or Baptist church. Amid the segregation and discrimination of the South, Morrison found comfort in the homes of strangers. She was especially struck by the familiarity she encountered among other blacks in the South, as if the community she knew in Lorain extended far beyond the borders of Ohio. While traveling with the Howard Players, she ate home-cooked meals that could have come from her grandmother's own kitchen.

Academically, Morrison discovered that Howard was a fairly conservative school. The undergraduate curriculum emphasized European history and culture and barely acknowledged the intellectual and literary contributions of African Americans. In an English class, she asked to write a paper on black characters in Shakespeare's plays. She later explained that the professor was "very much alarmed by that—horrified by it, thought it was a sort of lesser topic."[4] Her early interest in the way that white authors portray black characters would eventually culminate in the publication of her single book of literary criticism, *Playing in the Dark: Essays on Whiteness and the Literary Imagination* (1992), but that achievement was still decades away.

After completing her BA at Howard, Morrison studied at Cornell University, where she received a master's degree in English. Her thesis was titled "Virginia Woolf's and William Faulkner's Treatment of the Alienated." Her advisor, professor Robert Elias, recalled working with her, commenting that she was a "good student, not extraordinary, and she brought humor and compassion into her seminar work and commitment and a sharp focus." Elias was most impressed by her potential as a teacher, noting as well that "I didn't help her become a writer or not. My job was to make sure her writing was up to standard, which is a little ironic, you know."[5]

Morrison's thesis examines the ways in which Faulkner and Woolf address despair and suicide in their novels. The study adopts a moralistic tone as it seeks guidance from literary texts, rather than simply exploring their descriptions of human drama. This emphasis on the ways in which literature can help readers interact with others highlights a central concern of Morrison's fiction. Much like the novels of Faulkner, which are instructive and insightful without being overly didactic, Morrison's work seeks to present the complexities of social life in order to enhance how readers understand and operate in the world. Many critics have noted similarities between the novels of Morrison and those of Faulkner, commenting not only on their incisive analysis of race relations but also on their lyrical prose style. Morrison's initial attraction to Faulkner's work emanated from her admiration of his "refusal-to-look-away approach" as well as the outrage he inspired among readers and critics.[6] In her view, Faulkner is one of the few white American writers of his time period to take black people seriously.

While Morrison was at Cornell, the Supreme Court issued its landmark decision in the case of *Brown v. Board of Education of Topeka*. This ruling declared that "separate but equal" schools were unconstitutional, thus establishing the foundation for widespread social integration and galvanizing the emergent civil rights movement. Despite this historic decision, upon graduating from Cornell, Morrison faced an academic job market that was unaccustomed to considering, much less hiring, black faculty members. Her first teaching job was at Texas Southern University, a black college in Houston. In terms of curriculum, Morrison was here introduced to far more black history and culture than she had encountered at Howard. Black History Week, started in 1926 by Carter G. Woodson, was prominently celebrated at Texas Southern where there was a concerted effort to include aspects of African American history and culture in general courses.

After two years in Houston, Morrison returned to Howard in 1957 to teach English. Though Washington DC's level of segregation remained largely unchanged since she was a student, Morrison enjoyed other aspects of her time there. She became a mentor to the young Stokely Carmichael, who would later form the Student Nonviolent Coordinating Committee (SNCC), a key participant in the civil rights movement. Morrison remembers Carmichael as "the kind of student you always want in class—smart, perceptive, funny and a bit of a rogue. He *never* worked, and he stimulated all the others to think."[7] She also taught Claude Brown, author of *Manchild in the Promised Land* (1965), who approached her with an eight-hundred-page manuscript to read, an early version of his famous autobiographical novel. These informal mentor relationships anticipate Morrison's later dedication to young African American writers while she worked as an editor at Random

House. The following year, she married Harold Morrison, a Jamaican architect with whom she had two sons, Harold Ford and Slade Kevin.

During this time, Morrison joined a writing group that included the playwright and director Owen Dodson and painter Charles Sebree. The only requirement for the group was that each member had to bring something to share each week. After discarding various drafts she had started as a student, Morrison began writing about a young girl who wished for blue eyes; she named her Pecola Breedlove. Although Morrison derived the name of her tragic protagonist from the 1934 movie *Imitation of Life*, the inspiration for Pecola came from a real girl whom Morrison had encountered as a child. The girl once told her that she had definitive proof that God did not exist. The young Morrison listened to her companion explain that because she had prayed for blue eyes and had not received them, God was not real. Morrison imagined this girl with blue eyes and was horrified at the grotesque possibility. This story would eventually become her first novel, *The Bluest Eye*.

The 1960s were an especially tumultuous time in American history. In 1962, the Southern Christian Leadership Conference (SCLC) mobilized a campaign against segregation, first in Georgia and then in Alabama. A year later, Martin Luther King Jr. delivered his "I Have a Dream" speech on the steps of the Lincoln Memorial in Washington DC. The nonviolent protests of young black and white activists to desegregate the South were met with violence and brutality. In Mississippi three students were kidnapped and murdered during the summer of 1964 while countless others were beaten and intimidated simply for demanding equal rights. Despite ongoing stories of relentless violence and bigotry, significant gains were made including the passage of the Civil Rights Act in 1964 and the allocation of federal funds to create educational materials that would better reflect the ethnic diversity of the United States.

Although she followed the developments of the civil rights movement closely, Morrison did not engage in protests or marches herself. She was cautious about the stark realities of integration. Reflecting on the massive changes occurring nationwide, Morrison stated in a 1983 interview:

> Black people were thrown into contact with well-meaning white
> people, but also faced the ire and anger of those who were hostile
> to integration. Between the sudden intimacy with white people

on their side, so to speak, and the others, it threw people into great disarray.[8]

Morrison was concerned about maintaining the unique vitality of black communities in the face of integration. While the end of legal segregation was certainly a major achievement, it posed new challenges to preserving cultural practices and maintaining close social networks.

However, Morrison was equally skeptical of simplistic calls for "Black Power," an expression famously invoked by her former student Stokely Carmichael following the shooting of civil rights activist James Meredith in 1966. Black Power came to be associated with a range of beliefs and political goals including racial pride, the development of separate social institutions, and black autonomy. Morrison was especially critical of the slogan "Black is beautiful," arguing that it represents "a full concession that white definitions were important to us . . . and that the quest for physical beauty was both a good and worthwhile pursuit."[9] She claimed that such superficial beauty is a distraction "from what is worthy about us: for example, our intelligence, our resilience, our skill, our tenacity, irony or spiritual health."

Moreover, proponents of Black Power tended to emphasize the exotic over the real and often expelled or ignored critical aspects of black cultural history. Concerned with the consequences of promoting incomplete historical accounts, Morrison condemned the decision by the National Association for the Advancement of Colored People (NAACP) in 1963 to remove two statuettes of black jockeys that stood in the lobby of the Morrison Hotel in Chicago, the site of the group's annual national convention. While the NAACP leaders saw shame in the statuettes, Morrison reminded readers in a 1974 essay of the long and impressive history of African American horseracing. Cautious of the superficial call for Black Power, Morrison instead focused upon embracing the true roots and values of black culture, explaining:

> Before black life rearranged itself into elusive symbols of dashikis, pimp hats and kentecloth bikinis, we had a hold on life, an attitude which was most dramatically expressed in one particular area. This attitude was so strong and so familiar it never seemed to need definition—or never needed it until now when its death seems right at hand. It concerned work and the way we worked.

There was a press towards excellence in the execution of just about everything we tackled.[10]

These comments recall the fierce work ethic of George Wofford and the consummate integrity of Ella Ramah. While advocates of Black Power sought flamboyant symbols of African authenticity, Morrison urged blacks to rediscover strength in their families, in their communities, and, most importantly, in themselves.

Morrison's own self-reliance was put to the test when she discovered that once the initial romance of her marriage had faded, she and her husband had little in common, especially as he did not share her love of literature. In interviews, Morrison is notably reticent on the subject of her short-lived marriage, commenting that to discuss her divorce openly would only cause her children pain. She simply acknowledges, "He knew better about his life, but not about mine. I had to stop and say, let me start again and see what it is like to be a grown-up."[11]

After a trip to Europe with her then only son Harold, Morrison decided to leave her husband. Pregnant with her second son, she returned to her family in Lorain and settled her divorce in 1965. She never remarried, noting that there is significant freedom in being single and in discovering a way to live apart from the judgment of men. While many consider divorce a type of failure, Morrison has viewed her own as a key learning process that enabled her to stand up for herself. She credits her divorce for giving her the strength to ask for a raise that provided for the full care of her two children. Once asked if she would ever consider remarrying, Morrison quipped, "If I could find a guy with a big gun to shoot some people, then I might."[12]

A newly single mother with Slade on the way, Morrison took refuge in her parents' home before deciding what to do next. To the surprise of her family, she accepted a job at L.W. Singer, a textbook division of Random House based in Syracuse, New York. Hoping to make some changes in the ways that African Americans were represented in curriculum materials, she moved East with her two young sons. Although many were concerned that she would become lonely and depressed, Morrison had faith in the strength her family had already established within her. As she explains, "You take the village with you. There is no need for the community if you have a sense of it inside."[13]

Her mother did manage to track down a distant relative in the area, an old man who could hardly walk, but whose very presence provided Ramah with some degree of comfort that her youngest daughter was not entirely alone. While living in Syracuse, Morrison was confronted with many new challenges and experiences; she hired a white caretaker for her children and also initiated a $200,000 lawsuit against a neighbor who called her a tramp after complaining about the noise generated by Harold and Slade. The suit was eventually dropped. When life became especially difficult in upstate New York, Morrison most often thought of her grandmother Ardelia who escaped to Birmingham with her seven children. By comparison, her own life was more than manageable.

Isolated from family and friends and preoccupied with the care of her children, Morrison found writing to be a critical means to combat stress and loneliness; as she explains, "I never planned to be a writer. I was in a place where there was nobody I could talk to and have real conversations with."[14] Morrison's initial impulse toward writing was derived from a specific absence of community. While others in her situation might seek a new social circle or become wholly immersed in work and family responsibilities, Morrison sought another type of intimacy that was grounded in the exchange between reader, writer, and text. Apart from people with whom she could have "real conversations," Morrison began writing fiction, thus creating a new kind of dialogue and community. She later reflected:

> Once you leave home, the things that feed you are not available to you anymore, the *life* is not available to you anymore. And the American life, the *white* life, that's certainly not available to you. So you really have cut yourself off. Still, I can remember that world. I can savor it. I can write about it.[15]

Morrison's fiction is derived from a desire to establish the intimate world of family and community that she left behind in order to pursue her editorial career. Alone in upstate New York, she imagined new people to love and understand, and in this way she re-created the familiar network of support and strength of her childhood. However, many more years would pass before Morrison would share her writing with the outside world; her immediate focus at this time were her children and her rising editorial career.

Notes

1. Hilton Als, "Ghosts in the House: Profiles," *The New Yorker* (October 27, 2003): 68.

2. Bonnie Angelo, "The Pain of Being Black," *Time Magazine* (May 22, 1989): 120.

3. Adam Langer, "Star Power," in *Toni Morrison: Conversations*, ed. Carolyn C. Denard (Jackson, MS: University Press of Mississippi, 2008), 211.

4. Bessie W. Jones and Audrey Vinson. "An Interview with Toni Morrison," in *Conversations with Toni Morrison*, ed. Danille Taylor-Guthrie (Jackson, MS: University Press of Mississippi, 1994), 174.

5. Qtd. in Jim Haskins, *Toni Morrison: Telling a Tale Untold* (Brookfield, CT: Twenty-First Century Books, 2003), 41.

6. "Faulkner and Women," Faulkner and Yoknapatawpha Conference, in *Toni Morrison: Conversations*, ed. Carolyn C. Denard (Jackson, MS: University Press of Mississippi, 2008), 25.

7. Jean Strouse, "Toni Morrison's Black Magic," *Newsweek* (March 30, 1981): 56.

8. Rosemarie K. Lester, "An Interview with Toni Morrison, Hessian Radio Network, Frankfurt, West Germany," in *Critical Essays on Toni Morrison*, ed. Nellie Y. McKay (Boston: G.K. Hall & Co., 1988), 50.

9. "Rediscovering Black History," in *What Moves at the Margin: Selected Nonfiction*, ed. Carolyn C. Denard (Jackson, MS: University Press of Mississippi, 2008), 40.

10. Ibid., 52.

11. Elissa Schappell, "Toni Morrison: The Art of Fiction," in *Toni Morrison: Conversations*, ed. Carolyn C. Denard (Jackson, MS: University Press of Mississippi, 2008), 72.

12. Emily Bearn, "Toni Morrison: Voice of America's Conscience," *Times Online* (November 9, 2008).

13. Qtd. in Haskins, *Toni Morrison*, 51.

14. Jane Bakerman, "The Seams Can't Show: An Interview with Toni Morrison," in *Conversations with Toni Morrison*, ed. Danille Taylor-Guthrie (Jackson, MS: University Press of Mississippi, 1994), 30.

15. Colette Dowling, "The Song of Toni Morrison," in *Conversations with Toni Morrison*, ed. Danille Taylor-Guthrie (Jackson, MS: University Press of Mississippi, 1994), 58.

Chapter 3

EDITING AND MENTORSHIP

In 1968, Morrison moved to New York City to begin working at Random House's scholastic division. She decided on an apartment in Queens rather than in Manhattan so that she could keep a garden. Every morning she drove forty-five minutes into Manhattan, dropped off her sons at school, first the United National International School and then Walden School, and proceeded directly to her office. She picked her boys up when they were released from school at 3:30 and then drove back home. Later on, she started teaching a course on black women and contemporary literature at Yale on Fridays. Random House adjusted to her schedule as well as to her rather brash approach; as she explains, when it comes to establishing boundaries at work, "You don't ask, you just do."[1]

Interested in working in trade publishing, Morrison met with Robert Gottlieb, the editor in chief of Knopf, an imprint of Random House. Gottlieb recalls telling Morrison, "I like you too much to hire you, because in order to hire you I have to feel free to fire you. But I'd love to publish your books."[2] Gottlieb became her editor and worked with her through the publication of *Beloved* in 1987, while Morrison became a trade editor at Random House. The two continue to be close friends, and Morrison has long identified Gottlieb as one of her most valued readers, especially of early manuscript drafts. Her latest novel, *A Mercy*, is dedicated to him.

Morrison proved to be a diligent and inspiring editor. Although she had broad interests, editing books on topics as diverse as the women's movement and railroads, she focused primarily on developing young African American talent and promoting black publications. She worked with Quincy Troupe and Rainer Schulte on *Giant Talk* (1975), their anthology of Third World writing, and helped publish Ivan Van Sertima's *They Came Before Columbus: The African Presence in Ancient America,* which argues that Africans came to the New World centuries before Columbus in 1492. In 1974, the autobiography of scholar and activist Angela Davis was published under her guidance as was *Contemporary African Literature* (1972), a collection that included Wole Soyinka, Chinua Achebe, and Leopold-Sedar Senghor. Morrison hoped that the impressive color photographs of African tribesman and landscapes would increase sales, but unfortunately only a limited number of the books were sold. Additionally she edited the works of such writers as Henry Dumas, Gayl Jones, Lucille Clifton, and Toni Cade Bambara, nurturing the renaissance of black women's fiction that began in the 1970s. While working as an editor, Morrison observed that unlike black male authors, black women wrote with a fundamental sense of joy. Despite the difficulties of confronting daily acts of racism and sexism, writers like Clifton and Bambara explored the pleasure, comfort, and humor derived from existing in a community of vibrant black women.[3]

During the early 1970s, Black Studies and programs in African American history and culture were just beginning to appear in the university. Morrison's publishing efforts significantly contributed to the curriculum of these nascent programs, and ultimately her own novels would become some of the most frequent titles on course syllabi dedicated to both African American and American literary studies. Despite her fierce commitment to emerging black writers, Morrison has long insisted that black writers do not require black editors, noting that her own editors have been white men. Rather, she believes that the individual strengths and expertise of a particular editor are of paramount importance, not racial commonality.

In describing her work at Random House, Morrison has stated, "When I edit somebody else's book no vanity is involved. I simply want the writer to do the very best work he can do. Now if that means letting him alone, I'll do that. If it means holding hands, I'll hold hands. If it means fussing, I'll fuss."[4] Morrison's dedication to young black writers is especially apparent in her relationship with Gayl Jones. In 1973, Morrison received a massive box of manuscripts from one of Jones's teachers at Brown University. Morrison carefully waded through the vast trove of stories and full-length novels, including one that was over eight hundred pages. Amid these fragmented manuscripts, Morrison discovered the long short story that would eventually become Jones's first novel, *Corregidora* (1975), one of the most challenging and provocative works of contemporary American literature.

Morrison worked with the famously reclusive Jones, who was only in her early twenties at the time. One critic noted that "the title page of *Corregidora* should read, "by Gayl Jones, as told to Toni Morrison."[5] Morrison also took a risk with Jones's second book, a disturbing novel that is narrated by an institutionalized woman who castrates her lover. Like *Corregidora*, *Eva's Man* (1976) received impressive reviews—though many African American critics argued that both books foster negative images of the black community. Similar attacks would also be levied at *The Bluest Eye*, a text that demonstrates Morrison's firm commitment to exploring through fiction some of the most difficult issues affecting African Americans.

Morrison's desire to foster a more vibrant African American publishing community extended to her network of friends living in Queens, Harlem, and Brooklyn. Unlike Syracuse, the vibrant environs of New York City provided Morrison with a wide array of friends. She sought out other single mothers, many who were also pursuing a career in writing. She recalls periodically sending a little extra money to Toni Cade Bambara, who unasked brought groceries to her house and cooked dinner for Morrison and her children.

During this time, Morrison also befriended members of the Black Arts Movement such as Ishmael Reed, whose novel *Mumbo Jumbo* (1972) she edited, and Amiri Baraka, her former classmate at Howard. In describing the Black Arts Movement, which flourished during the late 1960s and early 1970s particularly in urban locations like Harlem, the scholar and social critic Larry Neal wrote:

> The Black Arts Movement is radically opposed to any concept of the artist that alienates him from his community. Black Art is the aesthetic and spiritual sister of the Black Power concept. As such,

it envisions an art that speaks directly to the needs and aspirations of Black America.[6]

Though Morrison agreed with the importance of generating politically conscious forms of artistic expression, she has long emphasized the need for literature to be both "unquestionably political and irrevocably beautiful at the same time."[7] Politically minded art can become propagandistic if it becomes divorced from the wonders of language and the surprise and variability of human emotions. From Morrison's perspective, literature should bear witness to history and to the stories that both nurture and critique community life.

Like the proponents of the Black Arts Movement, Morrison has worked to define and develop a uniquely black art, one that is not simply written by or about African Americans, but which reflects key aspects of black culture and history. She notes, for example, that "the way black people talk is not so much the use of non-standard grammar as it is the manipulation of metaphor."[8] While writers like Baraka emphasized establishing direct relationships to the community through poetry performances and community organizing, Morrison has sought to identify specific literary and thematic qualities that distinguish forms of African American narrative. Moreover, her commitment to the novel form emerges in part from her belief that music and oral storytelling no longer provide the black community with the narratives necessary to understand "what the conflicts are, what the problems are," though they "need not solve those problems." This approach demonstrates Morrison's core belief that narrative is fundamentally didactic; it teaches people how to organize knowledge and relate to others while also introducing readers to an assortment of complex characters.

According to Morrison, black art involves "the ability to be both print and oral literature." She links this oral quality to the experience of listening to a black preacher who inspires his congregation "to stand up and to weep and to cry and to accede or to change and to modify— to expand on the sermon that is being delivered." By emphasizing the response of readers and listeners, Morrison highlights her belief that literature must change lives and also that it exists as an evolving art form, which is influenced and developed by those who receive it. She explains, "It is the affective and participatory relationship between the artist or the speaker and the audience that is of primary importance," for it is here that art becomes truly transformative.[9] Literature should and must cause us to reevaluate and even restructure our lives. This interactive aspect of black art contributes to Morrison's belief that African American writers have a seemingly infinite variety of stories to tell. As she explains, "I think about what black writers do as having a quality of hunger and disturbance that never ends."[10]

A second critical aspect of black art, according to Morrison, is the presence of a choral voice, a community that observes and comments upon narrative action. She acknowledges that such a presence is not exclusive to African American work—it is evident in the Greek tragedies Morrison studied at Howard—but in emphasizing this collective voice, she underscores the key role that community plays in black life. This focus directly relates to Morrison's early experiences in Lorain. In her novels, she seeks to depict the same social network of care and concern that nurtured her as a child. However, her novels suggest that such a choral community of African Americans is not without faults or weaknesses.

Morrison also highlights the presence of ancestors as a key element of black art. She identifies ancestors as "sort of timeless people whose relationships to the characters are benevolent, instructive, and protective, and they provide a certain kind of wisdom." Some black writers like Richard Wright and James Baldwin write about struggles with an ancestral figure, but generally Morrison observes in these works that "It was the absence of an ancestor that was frightening, that was threatening, and it caused huge destruction and disarray in the work itself."[11] There are many ancestral figures apparent in Morrison's novels, but the most obvious is Pilate from *Song of Solomon*. This wise healer is grounded by her love for others, her deep connection to her familial history, and her utter disregard of social conventions. Her intimate relationship with her dead father and her expertise in folk practices emphasize forms of "discredited knowledge" that Morrison contends have been dismissed simply because of their association with black culture.[12] Black art, and novels in particular, must embrace the customs and values that have enabled African Americans to thrive under conditions of overwhelming oppression.

Morrison's frustration with aspects of the Black Arts Movement also reflects her concern that writers like Baraka, Eldridge Cleaver, and H. Rap Brown were far too concerned with issues of masculinity. She explains, "Those books and political slogans about power were addressed to white men trying to explain or prove something to them. The fight was between men, for king of the hill."[13] Along with writers like Alice Walker, Toni Cade Bambara, Gayl Jones, June Jordan, Lucille Clifton, Paule Marshall, and many others, Morrison was part of a late-twentieth-century renaissance in black women's literature. Despite significant differences in style and subject matter, these writers share a commitment to exploring the interrelated nature of oppressive social systems; racism, sexism, and classism do not operate in isolation but rather are deeply connected forms of discrimination and injustice. This literary flourishing was supplemented by the development of theoretical approaches to the experiences of black women. Academics and activists such as Patricia Hill Collins, Barbara Smith, Audre Lorde, and Barbara Christian began to explore the contours of black feminist thought. While celebrating the literary works of black women, they also sought to validate black female ways of knowing and to advance social change.

Morrison's commitment to developing black art also extended to efforts to preserve key aspects of African American history. In 1974, she published *The Black Book*, a type of archive of African American life. Although Morrison's name does not appear in the book, she was the impetus behind its creation. She developed the project out of a deep concern that the usable past was disappearing from African American communities. Her hope was to create a lasting monument to that history. Even as she realized that a book would be the best way to preserve this past, she aimed to have her work move beyond the limitations of a written document:

> Like every other book, it would be confined by a cover and limited to type. Nevertheless, it had to have—for want of a better word—a sound, a very special sound. A sound made up of all the elements that distinguished black life (its peculiar brand of irony, oppression, versatility, madness, joy, strength, shame, honor, triumph, grace and stillness) as well as those qualities that identi-

fied it with all of mankind (compassion, anger, foolishness, courage, self-deception and vision). And it must concentrate on life as lived—not as imagined—by the people: the anonymous men and women who speak in conventional histories only through their leaders.[14]

Morrison credits Middleton Spike Harris, a retired city employee with a massive collection of black memorabilia, as the primary author of *The Black Book*. Harris joined Morris Levitt, a retired public school teacher, Roger Thurman, director of New York's black New Heritage Repertory Theater, and Ernest Smith, owner of a resort on Lake George, to compile a vibrant archive of black culture from slavery to contemporary times. *The Black Book* includes photographs, newspaper clippings, drawings, advertisements, songs, letters, advice on interpreting dreams, voodoo recipes, and other documents.

Although not strictly chronological, the text opens with nineteenth-century notices concerning the sale of black slaves, a report on the slaves of Thomas Jefferson, a description of Joseph Cinque, leader of the *Amistad* revolt, and other clippings about antebellum history such as John Brown's raid on Harper's Ferry. Among these documents is an 1856 article titled "A Visit to the Slave Mother Who Killed Her Child." This report about Margaret Gardner, a slave woman who attempted to kill all four of her children in order to save them from being returned to slavery, would become the basis for Morrison's masterpiece, the novel *Beloved*. From the twentieth century, *The Black Book* includes a letter addressed to W. E. B. Du Bois, the eminent African American scholar and social critic who was the first black man to receive a PhD from Harvard. The letter is from a white professor conducting a study of crying and the expression of emotions. In formal, disturbingly detached prose, he asks Du Bois whether black people shed tears.

Morrison did not sign her name to the overview printed on the jacket of *The Black Book* though she authored the moving description:

I am *The Black Book*.

Between my top and my bottom, my right and my left, I hold what I have seen, what I have done, and what I have thought. I am everything I have hated: labor without harvest; death without honor; life without land or law. I am a black woman holding a white child in her arms singing to her own baby lying unattended in the grass.

I am all the ways I have failed: I am the black slave owner, the buyer of Golden Peacock Bleach crème and Dr. Palmer's Skin Whitener, the self-hating player of the dozens; I am my own nigger-joke.

I am all the ways I survived: I am tun-mush, hoecake cooked on a hoe; I am fourteen black jockeys winning the Kentucky Derby. I am the creator of hundreds of patented inventions; I am Lafitte the pirate and Marie Laveau. I am Bessie Smith winning a roller-skating contest; I am quilts and ironwork, fine carpentry and lace. I am the ways I fought, the gold I mined, the horses I broke, the trails I blazed.

Morrison's striking use of personification to describe *The Black Book* demonstrates her belief in the vitality of writing and reflects her conception of history as a living entity. The book embodies black men and women and does not romanticize or reinvent history, as Morrison suggests some purveyors of the Black Arts Movement did. Instead, the collection documents the totality of victories, failures, and survival that comprise African American life. It also draws upon the African American trope of the talking book, which black theorist Henry Louis Gates Jr. has identified as one of the most significant motifs in the black literary tradition. Morrison would develop this notion of the book as a human voice in her most stylistically ambitious novel, *Jazz*. Although Random House was skeptical of the entire project, fearing that it would not have a sufficient readership, *The Black Book* received significant praise both from reviewers and from individuals. Following its publication, Morrison received a letter from a man in prison who wrote to thank her and also to request additional copies.

Morrison encountered similar resistance to other projects she took on at Random House, including the promotion of Muhammad Ali's autobiography, *The Greatest* (1976). Most department stores refused to host the book-signing for fear there would be riots and looting. Once E. J. Korvette's agreed to sponsor the event, Morrison enlisted members of the Nation of Islam to act as peacekeepers throughout the rainy evening. She also directed an assistant to give Ali a baby when he became tired, knowing that babies always pacify the famous boxer. Under Morrison's masterful direction, the evening was an unqualified success with two thousand people in attendance.

Unfortunately, however, other difficulties arose following the release of *The Greatest*. The book had initially been conceived by the Nation of Islam as a way for Ali to respond to the accusation of draft evasion made by the U.S. government. Ali had refused to fight in the Vietnam War, citing his religious beliefs, but his statement "I ain't got no quarrel with them Viet Cong" caused a massive public outcry.[15] Morrison—like Richard Durham, who was hired as a coauthor for the book—hoped that the autobiography would delve into Ali's childhood growing up in a middle-class family in Louisville, Kentucky. However, Herbert Muhammad, the son of Nation of Islam leader Elijah Muhammad and the principal manager of Ali's career, insisted that the book be edited specifically to glorify the Nation of Islam and to sharpen the racism Ali encountered. Moreover, in a press conference that followed the book's publication, Ali admitted that he had not read the book, much to the embarrassment of his publisher and editor.

Despite this unfortunate encounter, Morrison generally enjoyed working with authors on a wide range of book projects. Her commitment to young black talent will likely continue to influence both popular and academic readers. For example, Morrison is largely responsible for publishing the work of Henry Dumas, a poet and short story writer who was shot in 1968 at the age of thirty-four by a transit cop in a New York City subway station. Upon the posthumous release of three of his books, Morrison wrote, "he had written some of the most beautiful, moving, and profound poetry and fiction that I have ever in my life read."[16] Though Dumas's books have not sold well since their initial publication, Morrison's praise and commitment to his writing will likely inspire young academics to rediscover his work.

Notes

1.   Colette Dowling, "The Song of Toni Morrison," in *Conversations with Toni Morrison*, ed. Danille Taylor-Guthrie (Jackson, MS: University Press of Mississippi, 1994), 54.

2.   Qtd. in Hilton Als, "Ghosts in the House: Profiles," *The New Yorker* (October 27, 2003): 70.

3.   Robert Stepto, "Intimate Things in Place: A Conversation with Toni Morrison," in *Conversations with Toni Morrison*, ed. Danille Taylor-Guthrie (Jackson, MS: University Press of Mississippi, 1994), 25.

4.   Jessica Harris, "I Will Always Be a Writer," in *What Moves at the Margin: Selected Nonfiction*, ed. Carolyn C. Denard (Jackson, MS: University Press of Mississippi, 2008), 8.

5.   D. Keith Mano, "How to Write Two First Novels with Your Knuckles," *Esquire* (December 1976): 62.

6.   Larry Neal, "The Black Arts Movement," in *The Portable Sixties Reader*, ed. Ann Charles (New York: Penguin Classics, 2003), 446.

7.   Toni Morrison, "Rootedness: The Ancestor as Foundation," in *What Moves at the Margin: Selected Nonfiction*, ed. Carolyn C. Denard (Jackson, MS: University Press of Mississippi, 2008), 64.

8.   Nellie McKay, "An Interview with Toni Morrison," in *Conversations with Toni Morrison*, ed. Danille Taylor-Guthrie (Jackson, MS: University Press of Mississippi, 1994), 152.

9.   Morrison, "Rootedness," 59.

10. McKay, "An Interview," 155.

11. Morrison, "Rootedness," 62.

12. Ibid., 61.

13. Jean Strouse, "Toni Morrison's Black Magic," *Newsweek* (March 30, 1981): 55.

14. Toni Morrison, "Rediscovering Black History," in *What Moves at the Margin: Selected Nonfiction, Toni Morrison*, ed. Carolyn C. Denard (Jackson, MS: University Press of Mississippi, 2008), 43.

15. Qtd. in Charles Lemert, *Muhammad Ali: Trickster in the Culture of Irony* (New York: Wiley Blackwell, 2003), 106.

16. Toni Morrison, "On Behalf of Henry Dumas," in *What Moves at the Margin: Selected Nonfiction*, ed. Carolyn C. Denard (Jackson, MS: University Press of Mississippi, 2008), 83.

Chapter 4

EARLY LITERARY CAREER

As Morrison has repeatedly stated, she wrote her first novel "in order to read it." This comment suggests that before committing pen to paper, she imagined herself as a reader, envisioning the books she wanted to read and the characters she wanted to know. Despite her prodigious study of literature, she was still hungry for books that described her experience and perspective as a black woman. At the time that Morrison began writing, the novels of such early twentieth-century black women writers as Zora Neale Hurston, Jessie Fauset, and Ann Petry were out of print. Morrison found greatest excitement in reading works by African writers like Chinua Achebe, Aime Cesaire, and Camara Laye who "did not explain their black world . . . [White writers] inhabited their world in a central position and everything nonwhite was 'other.' These African writers took their blackness as central and the whites were the 'other.'"[1] Morrison's admiration of this approach fundamentally influenced her lifelong commitment to writing for a black audience.

The genesis of Morrison's literary career is directly connected to her identity as a reader; amid the solitude of upstate New York, she sought the intimacy of books and the dialogue made possible through writing. The evolution of her novels demonstrates a sustained exploration of the deeply personal relationship involved in storytelling and of the transformative potential of reading. For Morrison, novels are sites of collaborative, intimate creation that teach and demand a participatory response from their audience. Because Morrison enjoyed the process of writing so much, she spent five years completing *The Bluest Eye*.

The first edition of *The Bluest Eye*, published by Holt, Rinehart & Winston in 1970, features a prominent picture of Morrison on the back cover. Wearing an afro, she looks directly at the camera. The front cover features no visual art but instead consists of the first two paragraphs of the novel. For readers to complete the opening sentence of the third paragraph, they must physically open the book. This structural device signals the importance Morrison places upon participatory reading; *The Bluest Eye*, like all of her subsequent novels, requires rigorous engagement on the part of its readers. The startling design of the book jacket heralds the arrival of a distinctive African American voice, one whose words demand immediate attention and whose back image defies the shame and self-hatred explored throughout the text.

Although *The Bluest Eye* was not a commercial success, its vibrant prose and courageous exploration of destructive American values attracted critical attention. In the *New York Times*, book critic John Leonard, who would eventually become one of Morrison's most ardent supporters as well as a close friend, wrote that Morrison's prose is "so precise, so faithful to speech and so charged with pain and wonder that the novel becomes poetry." Overwhelmed by the power of Morrison's language, Leonard notes that *The Bluest Eye* is more than fiction; it "is also history, sociology, folklore, nightmare and music."[2] The scope of Morrison's aim as well as the beauty of her language required a wholly new understanding of the reach and possibilities of literature. Here was fiction that moved beyond conventional notions of the literary to offer a new vision and understanding of African American life.

Exploring the origins and devastating consequences of racial self-hatred, Morrison focused her first novel on the most ignored member of society, a poor, black girl who longs for blue eyes. Pecola Breedlove believes herself to be ugly and accepts that beauty and virtue are only associated with whiteness. Although Morrison's description of Pecola's descent into insanity offers a pointed critique of white American values, the novel is primarily concerned with the health and responsibil-ities of the black community. Most significantly, Morrison set her artis-tic and critical gaze on black life; white characters are peripheral to the concerns, preoccupations, and joys of African Americans.

From the onset of her writing career, Morrison sought a form of address different from that used by other twentieth-century African American writers. Though she esteemed many of the works that have become pillars of the black literary canon, she was frustrated by their tone and condescending approach to black life:

> I was preoccupied with books by black people that approached the subject, but I always missed some intimacy, some direction, some voice. Ralph Ellison and Richard Wright—all of whose books I admire enormously—I didn't feel were telling me some-thing. I thought they were saying something about it or us that revealed something about us to you, to others, to white people, to men.

While Wright's *Native Son* (1940) and Ellison's *Invisible Man* (1952) explore relations between whites and blacks through the experiences of their male protagonists, Morrison's novels are distinguished by their close attention to dynamics within the black community and their emphasis on female experience. Morrison's characters, like Bigger Thomas and Invisible Man, are also subject to racist abuse and the pressures of a white-dominated society. However, their conflicts are examined within the context of a sharply delineated African Ameri-can world.

For example, although the Breedloves are profoundly influenced by white society, *The Bluest Eye* depicts how damaging conceptions of racialized beauty are perpetuated by blacks upon blacks and the result-ing crisis for the adolescent Pecola. This narrative approach marks a significant shift from some of the most influential mid-twentieth-century African American texts by exploring the inner workings of an independent and deeply complex black social structure. Upon reading *Invisible Man*, Morrison wondered, "Invisible to whom? Not me."[3] While Ellison's text encodes an awareness of a white observer into its very title, Morrison's works operate from the assumption of a black readership or of audience members willing to place themselves within the African American community.

Morrison begins *The Bluest Eye* by rehearsing a version of the Dick and Jane primers that gained enormous popularity in the 1940s. These stories, authored by William Elson and William Gray, portray an idealized version of American childhood grounded in a two-parent household and economic prosperity. This happy nuclear family was promulgated in the national media as an antidote to the hardships of the Great Depression and the instability of World War II. It became symbolic of a secure nation and the triumph of the American way of life. Morrison repeats a description of the Dick and Jane family three times. In the first, the text reads as expected with conventional punctuation. The second version is printed without any punctuation marks and lacks proper capitalization. The final version also dispenses with conventional grammar and is written with no spaces between the words.

The repeated use of the Dick and Jane story highlights how this conventional expectation of American life fails the two families most closely examined in *The Bluest Eye*, the MacTeers and the Breedloves. The happy nuclear family is a social myth built upon racial and class privilege. It represents a part of what Morrison has termed the "master narrative."[4] The master narrative refers to certain ideological constructs that we are taught to desire such as physical beauty based upon whiteness and a two-parent heterosexual household. The second two iterations of the Dick and Jane story may be understood as reflections of how that saccharine version of success is dangerously transposed upon the MacTeers and the Breedloves. The final version, with its words jammed together, represents the destructive chaos that emerges when especially disadvantaged black families aspire to an inevitably exclusive white ideal; the words become entangled, the story incoherent. *The Bluest Eye* describes a tragedy that at face value is beyond reason: the rape of a young girl by her father. Morrison's task is to find meaning in an act of such unrelenting horror. As Claudia, the novel's narrator, reflects in the first pages of the book, "There is really nothing more to say—except why. But since why is difficult to handle, one must take refuge in how" (6). Narrative, Morrison promises, will allow us to understand this evil and perhaps even empathize with those involved.

The opening line of *The Bluest Eye*, *"Quiet as it's kept, there were no marigolds the fall of 1941"* (5), introduces Morrison's abiding concern with the intimacy between reader and narrator. As she divulges a type of secret knowledge, the narrator speaks in a private, hushed voice to an audience that is consequently figured as a confidant, someone who is worthy of the trust necessary to comprehend the tragic story of a little girl's demise. Significantly, this first sentence does not directly mention the tragedy at the center of the novel, namely, Pecola's rape; rather the absence of the marigolds is the crucial secret, a natural aberration that the narrator then links to the story of Pecola. The secret involves a possible effect or symptom of Pecola's abuse. It is proof that something is wrong with the environment in which they live. This critical recognition that a force beyond Pecola is at work implies that she is not to blame for her tragedy. Because the telling of this story requires an audience sensitive to the failures of an entire community, the reader is warned to proceed with care and without prejudice.

In "Unspeakable Things Unspoken," Morrison elaborated on the tone she sought to capture in this opening sentence:

> First, it was a familiar phrase, familiar to me as a child listening to adults; to black women conversing with one another; telling a story, an anecdote, gossip about some one or event within the circle, the family, the neighborhood. The words are conspiratorial . . . It is a secret between us and a secret that is being kept from us. The conspiracy is both held and withheld, exposed and sustained. In some sense it was precisely what the act of writing the book was: the public exposure of a private confidence.[5]

By beginning *The Bluest Eye* with a divulged secret, Morrison establishes a crucial bond between reader and text. Moreover, by explicitly moving from an oral communication—a phrase she remembers first hearing—to a written exposition, she also signifies upon the tradition of "speakerly texts" in African American literature, a trope related to that of the talking book. According to Henry Louis Gates, Jr., "speakerly texts" are works "whose rhetorical strategy is designed to represent an oral literary tradition" thus generating the "illusion of oral narration."[6] What had been exchanged "within the circle, the family, the neighborhood" is now imparted to the reader in a form that threatens secrecy. The audience of *The Bluest Eye* is the privileged recipient of illicit information and must honor the trust and responsibility attendant in such a confession. Morrison further explains that such "instant intimacy seemed crucial to me then, writing my first novel. I did not want the reader to have time to wonder, "What do I have to do, to give up, in order to read this? What defense do I need, what distance maintain?"[7] Through her demand for "instant intimacy" from her readers, Morrison erases immediate differences between her audience and the novel's characters.

Elaborating on her desire to strip the reader of an identity apart from that created by the text, she has stated: "I would like to . . . put the reader into the position of being naked and quite vulnerable, nevertheless trusting, to rid him of all of his literary experience and all of his social experiences in order to engage him in the novel."[8] By assuming that readers can occupy an insider position in her texts, Morrison closes the gap created by socially mandated categories of identity such as race or class. In this way, she makes Pecola's story one to be shared within a circle of confidants, not scorned and dismissed by unsympathetic outsiders.

The opening of *The Bluest Eye* presupposes that the reader is part of the text's local African American community, and though this assumption may be erroneous, especially in light of Morrison's international eminence and her popularity among non–African American readers, it forces a type of creative collaboration between audience and text. Just as Claudia listens to Pecola's desire for blue eyes and Pecola in turn listens to the stories of the three local whores, so readers must participate in a text that assumes a willingness to hear and understand those individuals most ignored and despised by society. This demand for a highly engaged form of participation from the reader is not simply a matter of crossing racial barriers or establishing an intimacy based on shared cultural history. The story of *The Bluest Eye* requires a reader who is willing to empathize with characters rejected by society and able to comprehend horrific actions as manifestations of love. Commenting on how she wishes readers to perceive Cholly Breedlove, who rapes Pecola, Morrison reflects: "I want you to *look* at him and see his love for his daughter and his powerlessness to help her pain. By that time his embrace, the rape, is all the gift he has left."[9]

For Morrison, the intimacy between reader and text operates through a type of empathetic humanity and the struggle to perceive even the most atrocious acts as reflections, no matter how twisted and destructive, of love. She explains that her goal is to create between the reader and the text, "an intimacy that's so complete, it humanises him in the same way that the characters are humanised from within by a certain activity, and in the way in which I am humanised by the act of writing."[10] Morrison's comments suggest that in the world of her novels, the most vital connection is ultimately not between her fictional characters, but rather between the text and reader. Cholly is humanized only through the comprehension of individual readers and the intimacy established in the act of reading. One of Morrison's primary goals as a writer is to find humanity in horrifying actions and then to pass this insight on to her audience.

Although Cholly's rape of Pecola stands as the immediate atrocity of the novel, Morrison presents this devastating act alongside the systematic devaluation of black girls. Pecola's desire for blue eyes represents a pervasive self-hatred that affects the entire African American community. Only Claudia with the clarity of her youthful self-regard is able to recognize the outrageous error of giving white, blue-eyed dolls to black girls. When she receives this dubious gift, she understands that for the adults, "the doll represented what they thought was my fondest wish," but instead of instantly cuddling the new toy, Claudia is "physically revolted by and secretly frightened of those round moronic eyes, the pancake face, and orangeworms hair." She is possessed by a powerful desire to dismember the doll in order to "see of what it was made, to discover the dearness, to find the beauty, the desirability that had escaped me, but apparently only me."[11]

The doll defines beauty and therefore constitutes what is most beloved in society. Claudia recognizes that because the doll does not reflect her face and body, she has no social value; her skin bars her from the beauty treasured not only by white society but also by the black adults who give her the doll. Significantly, Claudia eventually comes to adore the white doll, learning to abide by the dominant mores of her society, for as she explains, "The best hiding place was love" (23). Her initial rage is powerless to combat the "master narrative" of white beauty, and thus she learns to delight in the image of Shirley Temple, the blue-eyed icon she can never become.

Unlike Claudia, Pecola accepts the conflation between whiteness, beauty, and love object without question. Claudia's initial disgust for the white dolls indicates a degree of self-esteem that is no doubt derived from her loving, stable parents. Pecola, however, has no such foundation of support and identity. She arrives at the Macteer house after her father, Cholly, is put in jail and the family is thrown out of their apartment. While her mother, Mrs. Breedlove, stays with the family that employs her as a maid, the two children are sent to separate foster homes. The Breedloves are distinguished not by their poverty, but by the fact that "No one could have convinced them that they were not relentlessly and aggressively ugly" (38). Each member of the family bears their ugliness in a distinctive way; Cholly channels his into violence, Mrs. Breedlove adopts hers as a form of martyrdom, their son Sammy uses his as a weapon to hurt others, and Pecola "hid behind hers. Concealed, veiled, eclipsed—peeping out from behind the shroud very seldom, and then only to yearn for the return of the mask" (39). Pecola understands that she is hateful in the eyes of others simply because she is female and black, and thus her only escape is through her abiding wish to become blue-eyed and hence beautiful.

Pecola is not the only character in the book to be negatively influenced by white conceptions of beauty. Pauline or Mrs. Breedlove, as her children call her, is also subject to the destructive consequences of yearning for a life from which she is fundamentally excluded. Because of a childhood accident, Pauline has a crooked foot that leaves her with a lifelong limp. Although her broken foot restricts her to domestic chores, it is key to her eventual marriage to Cholly. One day while leaning against a fence, she hears someone whistling behind her. As she enjoys the happy tune, she is surprised to feel someone touching her foot: "The whistler was bending down tickling her broken foot and kissing her leg. She could not stop her laughter—not until he looked up at her and she saw the Kentucky sun drenching the yellow, heavy-lidded eyes of Cholly Breedlove" (115). Cholly is delighted by Pauline's foot; what had been the symbol of her otherness becomes for him a point of endearment. The two head north to Lorain, Ohio, in search of better jobs, but their initial love turns sour as they struggle to make friends with suspicious blacks while avoiding the hostility of whites.

Pauline starts cleaning house in part to have money to buy the clothes and makeup she hopes will ingratiate her among the few black women she encounters. However, she loses her job one day when Cholly, drunk and demanding money, arrives at the home of Pauline's employer. The white woman fires Pauline because the latter refuses to leave Cholly and rejects her boss's offer to stay on at her house. Pauline reasons that *"it didn't seem none too bright for a black woman to leave a black man for a white woman"* (120). This exchange highlights the ways in which solidarity between black and white women can fail because of condescending attitudes about gender norms and simplistic approaches to the complexities of human relationships.

Soon after, Pauline becomes pregnant, much to Cholly's delight, and she stops working in order to prepare for the child. To escape the loneliness of the apartment, Pauline begins going to the movies:

> There in the dark her memory was refreshed, and she succumbed to earlier dreams. Along with the idea of romantic love, she was introduced to another—physical beauty. Probably the most destructive ideas in the history of human thought. Both originated in envy, thrived in insecurity, and ended in disillusion. In equating physical beauty with virtue, she stripped her mind, bound it, and collected self-contempt by the heap. . . . She was never able, after her education in the movies, to look at a face, and not assign it some category in the scale of absolute beauty, and the scale was one she absorbed in full from the silver screen. (122)

Though Pauline savors her afternoons in the movie theater, she soon discovers that "they made coming home hard, and looking at Cholly hard" (123). Against the standard of beauty and success depicted in the movies, their life is an absolute failure. Pauline comes to accept her ugliness and to resent Cholly, with whom she fights constantly. After the birth of her two children and due to Cholly's perpetual drunkenness, Pauline takes on the responsibility of bread-winner for the family. She becomes a stern and steady presence in church and channels all of her desire for beauty and order by becoming "an ideal servant" (127). While neglecting her own children and household, Pauline finds "Power, praise, and luxury" (128) in the home of her rich white employer. She jealously guards the joy of being part of this idyllic world, leaving her children to wallow in ugliness and the fear of a hopeless, despairing future.

While Pauline finds some stability and fulfillment in her job, Cholly remains dangerous precisely because he has no obligations—not to an employer and certainly not to his family. As the narrator explains:

> Cholly was free. Dangerously free. Free to feel whatever he felt—fear, guilt, shame, love, grief, pity. Free to be tender or violent, to whistle or weep. . . . Free to take a woman's insults, for his body had already conquered hers. Free even to knock her in the head, for he had already cradled that head in his arms. (160)

Cholly's profound sense of freedom stems from his early abandonment by his mother, who left him on a junk heap, and his rejection by his father, who dismisses him in order to continue playing a game of craps. Without a firm attachment to family or community, Cholly has nothing to lose and is thus free to be whatever he chooses; whether caring or violent to others, each approach is devoid of anything more than his own curiosity and personal desire. His two children perplex him because he has no model by which to relate to them, and thus his response to them is based entirely on his immediate sensations and frame of mind.

When Cholly returns home from a night of drinking and sees Pecola washing dishes, he is struck by "revulsion" at her "young, helpless, hopeless presence," and the "clear statement of her misery was an accusation" of his own failure and impotence (161). Overwhelmed by his guilt and pity, Cholly watches as Pecola raises one foot to scratch the back of her calf and recalls kissing Pauline's foot, the tender act that heralded their love. He repeats the action with his daughter and "the confused mixture of his memories of Pauline and the doing of a wild and forbidden thing excited him, and a bolt of desire ran down his genitals" (162). The narrator explains that Cholly's final emotion toward Pecola is love, and thus readers must consider how this violent act reflects some degree of care. Cholly gives to Pecola all that he has, namely, the power of his sex that once delighted Pauline. The rape is thus a grossly misguided demonstration of love and an act of frustrated impotence.

Already scorned for her ugliness, Pecola is entirely maligned after her mother finds her unconscious on the kitchen floor. Consequently, she falls prey to her earlier fantasy, believing that she has at last been granted blue eyes and that her beauty is responsible for her exclusion from others. Claudia observes Pecola's descent into madness and comes to understand that Pecola became a necessary scapegoat for the black community:

> All of us—all who knew her—felt so wholesome after we cleaned ourselves on her. We were so beautiful when we stood astride her ugliness. Her simplicity decorated us, her guilt sanctified us, her pain made us glow with health, her awkwardness made us think we had a sense of humor. Her inarticulateness made us believe we were eloquent. (205)

Claudia's concluding comments are a powerful indictment not simply of white social mores, which have already proved to be immensely destructive, but of the ways in which the black community promoted Pecola's ugliness and her exclusion from society. To return to the opening metaphor of the marigolds that did not bloom, the earth, like the town, is to blame. Pecola's tragedy reveals the failure not of a single family or even of one man, but of an entire community.

The Bluest Eye is now widely taught at both the college and the high school level, but its content so disturbed Morrison's sister Lois that she would not let her daughters read the book until they turned eighteen. With the money she earned from *The Bluest Eye*, Morrison announced plans to take her parents and children to Aruba. Ramah, however, had a deep fear of airplanes and insisted that she did not fly. But as there was no other way to get to the island, Morrison bought tickets for the flight. Ramah prepared for the trip and got on the plane. Later, Morrison asked her mother why she decided to come. Ramah explained, "I had a talk with my maker . . . And I told him, that if he was going to let me get up there in the airplane with my daughter and her family, and then was going to let it crash, I didn't want anything to do with his religion."[12] The trip marked the first time the whole family had been out of the country.

Morrison had taken on additional teaching positions at such universities as SUNY Purchase, Bard, Rutgers, and SUNY Albany when her second novel, *Sula*, was published in 1973. Nominated for a National Book Award and hailed by black feminist critic Hortense Spillers as "the

single most important irruption of black women's writing in our era,"
Sula describes the relationship between childhood friends Sula Peace
and Nel Wright.[13] Following the tragic demise of Pecola in *The Bluest
Eye*, this novel imagines the adult life of characters like Claudia and
Frieda, black women faced with the challenges of balancing family and
freedom, friendship and marriage. While Nel marries and settles into a
conventional life in the Midwestern Bottom community, Sula attends
college, travels, and becomes a social rebel. Upon her return home, Sula
is perceived as evil because she refuses to conform to traditional conventions and patterns of behavior. In this poignant novel of oppositions,
Morrison examines the interdependency between good and evil and the
complex relationships between black women.

In *Sula*, Morrison again provides a rich description of African
American community life, tempering the critique she offered in *The
Bluest Eye* to portray a vibrant though sharply judgmental collective.
Sula is set in the Bottom, an Ohio town situated in the rocky hills
above the all-white town of Medallion. By returning to a small Midwestern community, Morrison highlights her conviction that towns
are the epicenter of African American identity: "Most of our lives are
spent in little towns, little towns all throughout this country. And
that's where, you know, we live. . . . that's where we made it, not made
it in terms of success but made who we are."[14] The Bottom derives its
name from a "nigger joke" that begins when a white farmer promises
"a piece of bottom land" to his former slave in exchange for doing some
difficult work. When the slave completes the chores, the farmer
deceives him into believing that the valley land is less desirable than
the hills, which are "the bottom of heaven"[15] (5). The slave thus asks
for the infertile hill land. Despite this deception, the black settlers
build a prosperous town atop the difficult soil. This reversal from misfortune to success is emblematic of how Morrison engages with oppositions in the novel. Through various characters and themes, Morrison
posits a binary such as good and evil or life and death only to demonstrate how the duality collapses upon itself.

This play with opposition is most evident in the primary relationship of the novel, the friendship between Nel Wright and Sula Peace.
Reflecting upon the two characters in a 1976 interview, Morrison
noted that "if they had been one person, I suppose they would have

been a rather marvelous person. But each one lacked something that the other one had."[16] Nel is the only daughter of Helene, an upstanding member of the most conservative church in Medallion, and Wiley, who works as a ship cook and thus is hardly present in his daughter's life. Nel is raised in a strict though stable home that strongly contrasts with the disorder of Sula's family. Sula lives with her widowed mother, Hannah, her one-legged grandmother, Eva, and a collection of town misfits including a trio of orphaned boys that Eva each names Dewey and Tar Baby, a drunk who is reputably white. While Nel is taught to abide by proper social conventions, Sula learns at an early age that "sex was pleasant and frequent, but otherwise unremarkable" (44). Her mother sleeps with whoever interests her, but with such a lazy, carefree attitude that the women of the town take her flirtations with their husbands as a compliment rather than as a threat.

Eva also exemplifies this "manlove" but because of her physical handicap, she is limited to good-natured flirtations and to warning young wives to carefully tend to the desires of their husbands. Her advice to such women highlights her adherence to conventional gender roles despite the fact that she is one of the most independent and aggressive characters in the novel. However, this fierceness is solely derived from her maternal sensibility. In one of the most disturbing scenes of the novel, she sets her son Plum on fire after he returns from World War I, emotionally ravaged and addicted to drugs. Afraid that he will one day try to climb back inside her womb, she decides to let him die like a man. Eva is motivated by maternal love, but like Cholly in *The Bluest Eye*, her love is destructive, not healing. Love is again shown not to be an absolute value because it is always subject to the limitations of the lover. Eva's murder of Plum provides an important point of contrast to two later deaths witnessed by Sula that raise critical questions about the nature of responsibility and crime.

Despite their different upbringings, Sula and Nel become instant friends. The third-person narrator explains:

Because each had discovered years before that they were neither white nor male, and that all freedom and triumph was forbidden to them, they had set about creating something else to be. Their meeting was fortunate, for it let them use each other to grow on.

Daughters of distant mothers and incomprehensible fathers (Sula's because he was dead; Nel's because he wasn't), they found in each other's eyes the intimacy they were looking for. (52)

Their friendship allows both girls to blossom, providing them with the safety and courage to explore the world. Unlike the fearful Pecola or even the rule-bound Claudia, these girls experience a unique and generative sense of freedom. While Nel becomes the more stable and dependable of the two, Sula is marked by her recklessness. In one especially striking scene, she cuts off the tip of her finger to scare off a group of threatening Irish boys. This episode again reveals how Morrison undermines conventional oppositions in the novel. The boys presumably bear far greater social power because they are white and male. However, Sula inverts her lower social position by turning violence upon herself. By taking control of her own victimization, she ultimately bests the boys, who flee at the sight of her bloodied finger.

In the company of one another, Sula and Nel enjoy a profound strength. As young girls they parade themselves before a group of men and are pleased when local heartthrob Ajax pronounces them "Pig meat" (50). Although in certain circumstances this comment might be understood as threatening, it delights the girls precisely because of its raunchy connotations. Together they are free to experiment with their emerging sexuality and to explore the world around them with curiosity, not fear. However, this shared freedom also has dangerous repercussions. While playing with a local boy, Chicken Little, Sula loses her grip on his hands, sending him flying into the river. The girls watch as the water settles and Chicken does not reappear. They do not tell anyone of Chicken's death, and later when his body is found they attend his funeral, where Sula cries and Nel fears that someone will indict them for Chicken's death. As they stand before his grave, they recognize that while Chicken will abide in the earth, they will continue to live. They relax and with clasped hands return to their former adventures. Chicken's death suggests the dangers of freedom, much like the threat that Cholly posed to others due to his exaggerated independence.

Sula is a novel that revels in doubling, and with each set of paired characters or parallel scenes, Morrison provides new avenues of insight. For example, Chicken's death is followed by that of Hannah, who dies in an accidental fire. From an upstairs room, Eva watches the flames alight onto her daughter's dress and throws herself out the window in a desperate attempt to save Hannah. Eva survives the fall and is subsequently haunted by the vision of Sula watching her mother burn alive from the porch. While others attribute Sula's response to shock, Eva believes that her granddaughter watched out of perverse curiosity. As in the case of Chicken, Sula observes death from a peculiar state of detachment. This unsettling separation from others highlights her emerging sense of independence and her refusal to fulfill any familial or social obligations. After ten years of travel, Sula returns to the Bottom to tell Eva, "Don't talk to me about how much you gave me, Big Mamma, and how much I owe you or none of that. . . . I don't want to make somebody else. I want to make myself" (92). Focused entirely upon the satisfaction of her own desires, Sula rejects Eva's mandate to settle down and have children and to the consternation of the Bottom community she eventually sends her grandmother to a nursing home.

Despite Sula's heightened sense of self, she retains a firm commitment to Nel, who stays in the Bottom, becoming a dutiful mother and housewife. Upon Sula's return, the two rediscover their former camaraderie. As Nel reflects, "Sula. Who made her laugh, who made her see old things with new eyes, in whose presence she felt clever, gentle and a little raunchy" (95). Sula injects new life and, most importantly, humor in Nel's conventional life. However, their friendship is destroyed when Sula sleeps with Jude, Nel's husband. Nel cannot forgive this betrayal, though for Sula the act was not one of malice but of mere curiosity: "She had no thought at all of causing Nel pain when she bedded down with Jude. They had always shared the affection of other people: compared how a boy kissed, what line he used with one and then the other" (119). Sula assumes that the bond between herself and Nel is so strong that marriage should pose no impediment to their intimacy. In Sula's mind, the relationship between them is primary, and thus Nel is deceived in believing that Jude provides some greater love or support. Nel's response reveals to Sula that they are now irrevocably split: "She had clung to Nel as the closest thing to both an other and a self, only to discover that she and Nel were not one and the same thing" (119). While Nel accepts the conventions of marriage and prescribed gender roles, Sula continues to live apart from all social expectations.

The intensity of the relationship between Nel and Sula has led some critics, most notably Barbara Smith, to read the text as a "lesbian novel."[17] Morrison claims that this interpretation discredits the novel's central focus on Nel and Sula's friendship.[18] Her aim in the novel was to describe the emotional support that black women have always provided for one another, a neglected topic that is often dismissed due to a general overemphasis on heterosexual relationships. As she explains, "Friendship between women is special, different, and has never been depicted as the major focus of a novel before *Sula*."[19] However, in labeling the novel "lesbian," Smith did not simply mean to imply that Sula and Nel are sexually attracted to one another. Rather, she argues that the text "works as a lesbian novel not only because of the passionate friendship between Sula and Nel but because of Morrison's consistently critical stance toward the heterosexual institutions of male-female relationships, marriage, and the family."[20] In Smith's reading, the novel is lesbian because it depicts women who identify most strongly with other women and also because it demonstrates that female sexual pleasure is constrained, not liberated, by marriage.

Nel, for example, cannot conceive of sex outside the confines of marriage, viewing her thighs as "empty and dead" following Jude's departure (110). She relies upon her adulterous husband for a sexual identity rather than discovering what black feminist critic and activist Audre Lorde termed the power of "the erotic" within her. Lorde described "the erotic" as "an assertion of the lifeforce of women; of that creative energy empowered."[21] Sula fully indulges in her erotic power as she relishes sexual encounters with men. In vivid prose, Morrison describes Sula's eroticism as a way to discover her own creativity. She imagines her lover, Ajax, as a series of layers—bone giving way to gold and alabaster and finally to loam—that she uncovers as she comes to sexual climax. For Sula, sex is a vehicle of self-exploration, while for Nel it is exclusively bound to the institution of marriage and the pleasure of her husband. Between such opposing perspectives, there is no middle ground by which the former friends can reconcile their differences.

In the final scene of the novel, Nel visits the aged and somewhat delusional Eva. The elder woman asks about the death of Chicken:

"How did you get him to go in the water?"

"I didn't throw no little boy in the river. That was Sula."

"You. Sula. What's the difference? You was there. You watched, didn't you?

Me, I never would've watched." (168)

Despite their significant differences, Eva suggests there is no distinction between Nel and Sula because of their shared culpability in Chicken's death. The comment jolts Nel into an awareness of the friend she has lost, the one who might help her understand Eva's comment as well as her accusation. The novel concludes with Nel's recognition that "All that time, all that time, I thought I was missing Jude. . . . We was girls together" (174). She at last understands that Sula had been her most intimate confidant and that their love was more nurturing than what Jude ever provided.

Despite the novel's primary focus on Sula and Nel, the book opens with a description of Shadrack, a World War I veteran who returns severely traumatized from the violence and destruction he witnessed abroad. Shadrack lives largely as an outcast from others, but he does engage with the Bottom community in one key way. In his struggle to find order in a world prone to violence and chaos, he decides to make a space for fear as a way of controlling it:

> It was not death or dying that frightened him, but the unexpectedness of both. In sorting it all out, he hit on the notion that if one day a year were devoted to it, everybody could get it out of the way and the rest of the year would be safe and free. In this manner he instituted national Suicide Day. (14)

Every January 3, a date historically associated with the start of the annual antebellum slave market, Shadrack calls out to the people of the Bottom with his cowbell, "Telling them that this was their only chance to kill themselves or each other" (14). Although the townspeople are at first frightened by Shadrack, they eventually come to incorporate National Suicide Day into their annual routine. They accept his madness, in part because Shadrack is a noisy but ultimately harmless presence.

This attitude toward Shadrack's bizarre behavior is critical to Morrison's depiction of the African American community in *Sula*. She explains:

Black people never annihilate evil. They don't run it out of their neighborhoods, chop it up, or burn it up. They don't have witch hangings. They accept it . . . It's as though God has four faces for them—not just the Trinity, but four.[22]

This acceptance of the inevitability of evil explains how the people of the Bottom respond to Sula. As a woman who throws her grandmother into a nursing home and who is rumored to sleep with white men, she threatens basic moral tenets and social conventions. However, the community does not attack Sula, believing instead that the "presence of evil was something to be first recognized, then dealt with, survived, outwitted, triumphed over" (118).

Consistent with the play with oppositions that functions throughout the novel, Morrison demonstrates how Sula's presence in the Bottom actually improves the community. For example, Sula's loose ways and disregard of familial bonds inspires a derelict mother to reform her lifestyle and care for her son. Using Sula as a key point of contrast, the townspeople "began to cherish their husbands and wives, protect their children, repair their homes and in general band together against the devil in their midst" (117–18). The evil that Sula represents ultimately acts as a force of good for the community. This inversion highlights Morrison's contention that "one can never really define good and evil. Sometimes good looks like evil; sometimes evil looks like good—you never really know what it is. It depends on what uses you put it to. Evil is as useful as good is."[23]

Sula comes to recognize the permeability of good and evil in her final encounter with Nel.

"How you know?" Sula asked.

"Know what?" Nel still wouldn't look at her.

"About who was good. How you know it was you?"

"What you mean?"

"I mean maybe it wasn't you. Maybe it was me." (146)

Nel is deemed good because she adheres to the values and beliefs of the Bottom community. However, Sula arguably has a more positive influence upon the townspeople by inspiring them to act against the evil she reputably represents. Moreover, Nel's uncritical acceptance of the institution of marriage and the primacy placed upon heterosexual union prevents her not only from experiencing the full possibilities of sexual pleasure but also from preserving her relationship with Sula. Morrison demonstrates that the creation of strict dualities only limits our understanding of how people operate as complex, multifaceted beings. Oppositions between good and evil, black and white, self and other ultimately collapse upon themselves. Though we may rely upon such labels as neat categories of identity, they restrict our ability to understand the dynamic nature of human motivations.

With *Sula*, Morrison felt that she had developed a distinctive voice and style of her own. However, she would not begin calling herself a writer until after the publication of *Song of Solomon*. Following the completion of *Sula*, Morrison fell into a minor depression because she missed the characters of her second novel. However, inspiration soon returned and she began work on her third book. Published in 1977, *Song of Solomon* received massive critical acclaim. A national best-seller, it won the National Book Critics Award and was the first African American Book of the Month Club selection since *Native Son* in 1940. Drawing upon black folklore as well as biblical stories, Morrison explores mythic themes of flight, family, and responsibility while offering a fundamental ethos of hope and love. Along with *Beloved*, it has been hailed as one of her unequivocal masterpieces and it is among the favorite novels of President Barack Obama.

Song of Solomon represents a significant shift in subject matter for Morrison. While *The Bluest Eye* and *Sula* focus primarily on female characters and dynamics between women, *Song of Solomon* is fundamentally concerned with the development of a black man. In describing Milkman Dead's epic quest for identity, Morrison discovered that she needed to use new metaphors than those that animated her previous novels. As she explained in a 1977 interview:

> I needed something that suggested dominion—a different kind of drive. I think *Song* is more expansive because of that; I had to loosen up. I could not create the same kind of enclosed world that I had in previous books. . . . It's a feminine concept—things happening in a room, a house. That's where we live, in houses. Men don't live in those houses, they really don't.[24]

In order to capture Milkman's transformative journey for cultural knowledge and understanding, Morrison turned to the myth of the flying Africans. According to black folklore, a group of slaves escaped bondage in the American South by flying home to Africa. This story, which has roots in Yoruba legend, has been titled "All God's Chillun Had Wings" and was first recorded in *Drums and Shadows: Survival Studies among the Georgia Coastal Negroes,* a book produced in the early 1900s by the Federal Writers' Project. Morrison relies upon flight as one of the central motifs of *Song of Solomon,* exploring how it signals freedom yet inevitably leads to abandonment. She alludes to this tension in the novel's epigraph, which reads, "The fathers may soar/ And the children may know their names." While most epigraphs are derived from well-known literary sources, Morrison with customary bravado opens her novel with a phrase that she penned herself. The epigraph links flight to masculinity, for it is the "fathers" who soar and the children who, while knowing their names, may not know them with much intimacy due to their absence. The flying Africans who escaped slavery left grieved family members behind but also a magnificent legacy of transcendent possibilities.

The epigraph also introduces another key theme of the novel—naming. In the opening chapter, Morrison explains how the African American community of an unnamed Michigan town, where *Song of Solomon* is set, uses names as a form of resistance against white society. For example, the townspeople initially refer to the street where the only black doctor lived as Doctor Street despite being officially registered as Mains Avenue. In an attempt to end the confusion caused between the two names, one indicative of black pride in Dr. Foster's achievements and the other a title with no organic link to the community, a notice is posted stating that the street is to "be known as Mains Avenue and not Doctor Street."[25] The black residents thus proceed to call the street "Not Doctor Street," complying with the edict while also flaunting white attempts to control their community. Similarly, the townspeople refer to Mercy Hospital as No Mercy Hospital because until the day that Milkman Dead is born, the opening day of the novel and also Morrison's own birthday, no blacks are allowed to seek care there. The convergence of Milkman's birth date with that of Morrison suggests that this black man's bildungsroman is also applicable to women.

The humorous reversal of names, explicated in the novel's opening chapter, follows the African American tradition of signifying which involves verbal play such that a new meaning is created through repetition with a difference. The names Not Doctor Street and No Mercy Hospital indict the false dominion and hypocrisy of white society while also preserving the history of this African American community. The names of the characters in *Song of Solomon* are either derived from a story that provides insight into the past or used to signify upon conventional biblical allusions. In the case of Pilate, Milkman's wise aunt, both forms of meaning are apparent.

Pilate, who was born without a navel and is one of Morrison's most memorable characters, is named by her father, Macon Dead Senior, who maintains the family tradition of picking a name blind from the Bible. The attending midwife warns that Pilate is the man who sentenced Christ to death, but Macon, illiterate and grieved by the death of his wife in childbirth, "chose a group of letters that seemed to him strong and handsome; saw in them a large figure that looked like a tree hanging in some princely but protective way over a row of smaller trees" (18). For Macon, the look of the word is more important than its conventional associations. This distinction emphasizes that literacy and traditional forms of knowledge are limited ways by which to understand the world. Pilate represents a key ancestral figure in the text. As a healer and communicator with the dead, she embodies what Morrison terms "discredited forms of knowledge." Despite the negative associations with her name, she dies wishing that she could have known more people because "If I'd a knowed more, I would a loved more" (336). In this way, Morrison signifies upon the original meaning of the name Pilate and highlights its aural quality. As will be further discussed, she represents a form of flight that operates through love rather than through physical departure; she is the true "pilot" of the novel.

As she explores the process and dynamics of naming in *Song of Solomon*, Morrison directly responds to the trauma caused by the eradication of identity and family history enacted by slavery:

> I never knew the real names of my father's friends. Still don't. They used other names. A part of that had to do with cultural orphanage, part of it with the rejection of the name given to

them under circumstances not of their choosing. If you come from Africa, your name is gone. It is particularly problematic because it is not just your name but your family, your tribe. When you die, how can you connect with your ancestors if you have lost your name? That's a huge psychological scar. The best thing you can do is take another name which is yours because it reflects something about you or your own choice.[26]

Names in *Song of Solomon* are laden with meaning. Milkman's best friend, Guitar, is named for the object his family could not afford to give him as a child. The family name, Dead, refers to a mistake made by a drunken clerk at the Freedman's Bureau, and Milkman, though named after his father and grandfather, goes by the nickname that alludes to his mother's practice of nursing him until he was a grown boy.

The title *Song of Solomon* refers both to the children's rhyme that leads Milkman to discover that he is descended from the flying African, Solomon, and to the twenty-second book of the Old Testament. The biblical text, also called the Song of Songs, is a collection of lyrical exchanges between two lovers. The lovers are reputedly King Solomon, who was renowned for his wisdom, and a Shulamite woman who is possibly the legendary queen of Sheba. The biblical Song of Solomon is notable for its sensual language and powerful imagery that explores love as a life-sustaining force that extends beyond individuals to encompass all of nature. The text's most famous line reads in the King James Bible as "I am black but comely," highlighting the African origin of the woman. However, later scholars have argued that the original Hebrew is better translated as "black and comely" and thus does not imply an opposition between beauty and blackness.

Many aspects of the Dead family reflect Morrison's own history. The practice of choosing a child's name at random from the Bible is how Ramah received her name. Moreover, the lyrics that the children sing in the concluding chapters of the novel and which lead Milkman to discover the history of his great-grandfather Solomon are based on a song from Morrison's family that begins, "Green, the only son of Solomon." The original song is followed by words that Morrison did not understand but which map out a genealogy just like the lyrics she generated for the novel. Much of the inspiration for *Song of Solomon* was derived from Morrison's grief following the death of her father. She cites the conversations she had with him in her head as critical to her growing understanding of how men function in the world. Like Pilate, who converses with her dead father and continues to be guided by his life, Morrison also drew upon her close relationship with her father to create this soaring novel.

Milkman, the privileged son of a materialistic father and a troubled mother, spends much of the novel in a state of suspended childhood. Coddled by his two older sisters—Magdalena, called Lena, and First Corinthians—he has little desire to do anything but get drunk, have sex, and superficially differentiate himself from his domineering father. Macon Dead commands his son to "own things. And let the things you own own other things. Then you'll own yourself and other people too" (55). Having watched his father shot by white men who coveted his family's farm, Macon believes that power resides entirely in the accumulation of wealth. He has the courage to request permission to woo Ruth Foster, the daughter of the only black doctor in town, because of the growing number of tenant houses he owns. Macon proves to be a greedy and inflexible landlord; he evicts Guitar's grandmother and the children she is raising by herself. Estranged from his community, distant with his children, and disgusted by his wife, Macon represents the spiritual emptiness of a life dedicated entirely to the accumulation of material wealth. Though he longs for greater intimacy, he is ashamed by Pilate's unconventional behavior and cannot move past his revulsion for Ruth.

Macon marries his wife not for love but because of her social status and the wealth he stands to inherit from her. Although their relationship begins with some degree of mutual attraction, Macon becomes increasingly disturbed by Ruth's excessive attachment to her father. He protests Dr. Foster's decision to oversee the birth of Lena and First Corinthians and is frustrated by his father-in-law's dismissive attitude toward the tenant properties he owns. However, Macon becomes permanently disgusted by his wife when he finds her in bed naked beside Dr. Foster's corpse with his fingers in her mouth. Later this scene is described to Milkman from Ruth's perspective, and she claims that she had been wearing a slip and was kissing her father's fingers, the only part of him that was not ravaged by disease.

Macon, however, is left to wonder if his wife had been carrying on an incestuous relationship with her father though he is confident that due to his father-in-law's addiction to ether, they would have been unable to engage in intercourse. Consequently, Macon stops having sex with Ruth, who, starved for physical contact, seeks Pilate's help to lure her husband back to her bed. Pilate gives Ruth something to mix into Macon's food, and soon he is drawn back to his wife, who becomes pregnant with Milkman. Abandoned by her husband, Ruth nurses her son well past the age at which children are typically weaned. A self-described "small woman" who is "small because I was pressed small," Ruth lives a sheltered existence that is punctuated by minor joys such as the water mark that commemorates her father's insistence on a decoration for the dining table and her ability to still inspire Macon's rage if not other forms of his attention (124).

Milkman is largely oblivious to the tension between his parents, and when he eventually learns the root of Macon's hatred for Ruth as well as the circumstances of his birth from his mother, he is irritated, wanting "to escape what he knew, escape the implications of what he had been told." He concludes that "None of that was his fault, and he didn't want to have to think or be or do something about any of it" (120). This refusal to take an interest much less responsibility for the past is emblematic of Milkman's prolonged childhood. Without a strong connection to his family or an understanding of his cultural history, Milkman is an aimless and narcissistic drifter. His spiritual deficiency is illustrated by the fact that one of his legs is shorter than the other, causing him to walk with a stiff-legged strut. This affectation hides the truth of his inner imbalance much like his face, which "lacked coherence, a coming together of the features into a total self" (69).

Milkman carries on a lengthy affair with Pilate's granddaughter, Hagar, that highlights his careless disregard of others. Inspired by youthful thrill, Milkman initially relishes sex with his older, vaguely mysterious cousin. However, he eventually becomes bored, describing her as "the third beer . . . the one you drink because it's there, because it can't hurt, and because what difference does it make" (91). As Milkman's affection wanes, Hagar becomes increasingly devoted. Though marriage is impossible for them, Milkman ends the relationship callously and Hagar, infuriated, takes to plotting his murder each month. A clumsy and brokenhearted killer, Hagar is unable to hurt Milkman, who cruelly dismisses her.

Milkman's only meaningful relationship is with his best friend, Guitar. Street-savvy and insightful, Guitar first introduces Milkman to Pilate. The two share a rambunctious adolescence, but as adults they embark on opposite paths. While Milkman is content to go "wherever the party is," Guitar stops drinking and becomes especially concerned with the rampant violence against blacks plaguing the nation (106). The lynching of Emmett Till, a teenage boy who dared to whistle at a white woman, leads Guitar to join a secret society of black men called the Seven Days. The Days are dedicated to "keep(ing) the numbers the same" in the seemingly endless procession of racial violence (154). Guitar explains:

> When a Negro child, Negro woman, or Negro man is killed by whites and nothing is done about it by their law and their courts, this society selects a similar victim at random, and they execute him or her in a similar manner if they can. If the Negro was hanged, they hang; if a Negro was burnt, they burn; raped and murdered, they rape and murder. (154–55)

Milkman is astounded by Guitar's involvement and concerned that the murder of any person will irrevocably change his friend. Moreover, he notes that by being in the Seven Days, Guitar cannot have a family or children, concluding, "There's no love in it." Guitar responds by stating, "What I'm doing ain't about hating white people. It's about loving us. About loving you. My whole life is love" (159). Every member of the group is assigned a different day of the week and is responsible for equalizing the violence that befalls black people on that day. As the Sunday man, Guitar stumbles into difficulty when four black girls are killed in a bombing at a Birmingham church, an actual event that occurred in 1963. His need to secure explosives to replicate the death of four white girls leads him to join Milkman in chasing after a cache of gold that Macon believes Pilate stole and hid when they were children.

Milkman and Guitar initially break into Pilate's house, believing that the gold is hanging from the ceiling in a green sack that Pilate refers to as her "inheritance" (163). In fact, the bag holds a collection of human bones that are eventually revealed to belong to her father, Macon Senior. Neither Milkman nor Guitar regrets the mistake nor apologizes to Pilate for the theft; both are so blinded by their quest for gold that they disregard all that Pilate has done for them. Although Milkman has no immediate need for money, he traces Pilate's history, first to Pennsylvania and later to the South, in order to find the gold his father insists Pilate has hidden. Retrieving the treasure represents his only act of independence, and he foolishly believes that by tracking it down he will feel some greater satisfaction with his wayward life. However, while his pursuit of the gold proves fruitless, through his journey to the South Milkman discovers something of far greater value—knowledge of his family history.

Milkman undertakes his trip to find the gold by himself despite Guitar's uneasy response to this decision. Suspicious that Milkman may be cutting him out of his share, Guitar follows him and later becomes convinced of his mistrust. Milkman's journey to the South is marked by his increased understanding of his forefathers. He learns of the deep admiration accorded to his father, Macon Dead, "who was strong as an ox, could ride bareback and barefoot, who, they agreed, outran, outplowed, outshot, outpicked, outrode them all." Milkman struggles to "recognize that stern, greedy, unloving man in the boy they talked about, but he loved the boy they described and that boy's father" (234–35). Although Milkman's search for the gold is futile, his interest in learning about his family history and the culture of the South grows. Initially, he offends a group of men in the town of Shalimar by carelessly flaunting his wealth and asking about the women without introducing himself. However, after a brief physical fight with a younger man, Milkman is welcomed to accompany a group of hunters on a night escapade.

The midnight chase after a bobcat physically exhausts Milkman but teaches him that his material possessions are useless in this world. Shedding his former self, he relishes the fraternity among the hunters, the exhilaration of their mission, and their visceral communication through the woods which he understand as "what there was before language. Before things were written down" (278). The journey also causes Milkman to reflect more deeply about the people in his life. For the first time, he considers the rejection Ruth has long endured, the grief and rage that has fostered his father's materialism, the disregard with which he treated Hagar, and the grave offense he committed in attempting to steal from Pilate.

Newly attentive to the sounds around him, Milkman returns to town, and while listening to the lyrics sung by a group of children, he realizes that the song is about his own great-grandfather, Solomon, who flew back to Africa.

Jake the only son of Solomon
Come booba yalle, come booba tambee
Whirled about and touched the sun
Come konka yalle, come konka tambee

Left that baby in a white man's house
Come booba yalle, come booba tambee
Heddy took him to a red man's house
Come konka yalle, come konka tambee

The song concludes, "Solomon done, fly, Solomon done gone/ Solomon cut across the sky, Solomon gone home" (303). Milkman exults over his sudden understanding of his family's history, and he heads back to Michigan, thrilled to share his news with Pilate. She, however, attacks him with a bottle and throws him in the cellar as punishment for the death of Hagar. Distraught over his rejection, Hagar sinks into a depression that ends in her death. While Milkman was reveling in the joys of his flight to the South, a woman suffered in his absence. This dynamic parallels the contrast between Solomon's flight to freedom and the wild grief experienced by Ryna, his wife; flight is glorious and enriching, but someone is inevitably left behind.

Milkman takes Pilate to Shalimar, where together they at last bury the bones of her father. As they finish, Pilate falls, shot by Guitar. Milkman sings to her as she dies, understanding the depth of his love and admiration for her because "Without ever leaving the ground, she could fly" (336). Pilate's desire to love all of those around her represents another form of flight, one that is not based on physical departure or individual achievement; instead it finds fulfillment in meaningful relationships. Pilate's flight is derived not from a struggle for personal independence, but from a commitment to loving others.

The novel ends as Guitar emerges from the wilderness; dropping his gun, he confronts Milkman, ready for physical combat. Milkman "wheeled toward Guitar and it did not matter which one of them would give up his ghost in the killing arms of his brother. For now he knew what Shalimar knew: If you surrendered to the air, you could *ride it*" (337). Milkman's death is irrelevant to the greater recognition of his own ability to fly. However, Morrison still leaves readers with a notably ambiguous conclusion because it is not clear what is the nature of Milkman's flight. Has he learned to physically fly like Solomon or has he embraced Pilate's model of flight in which love liberates him from his own body? Does he confront Guitar with such love or with a miraculous new power that will slay his former friend? Morrison's refusal to provide a clear response to these issues only widens our understanding of what flight means and how it may affect others. As in her previous two novels, Morrison concludes *Song of Solomon* by placing the responsibility of interpretation upon her audience. Just as readers of *The Bluest Eye* are challenged to question their own part in Pecola's demise, those completing *Song of Solomon* are left to ponder the fates of both Milkman and Guitar. By requiring a participatory relationship with her readers, Morrison compels her audience to complete the stories she begins.

Notes

1.   Claudia Dreifus, "Chloe Wofford Talks about Toni Morrison," in *Toni Morrison: Conversations*, ed. Carolyn C. Denard (Jackson, MS: University Press of Mississippi, 2008), 102.

2.   John Leonard, "Review of *The Bluest Eye*," *New York Times* (November 13, 1970).

3.   Pam Houston, "Pam Houston Talks with Toni Morrison," in *Toni Morrison: Conversations*, ed. Carolyn C. Denard (Jackson, MS: University Press of Mississippi, 2008), 253

4.   Bill Moyers, "A Conversation with Toni Morrison," in *Conversations with Toni Morrison*, ed. Danille Taylor-Guthrie (Jackson, MS: University Press of Mississippi, 1994), 262.

5.   Toni Morrison, "Unspeakable Things Unspoken: The Afro-American Presence in American Literature," in *The Norton Anthology of African American Literature*, 2nd ed., ed. Henry Louis Gates Jr. and Nellie Y. McKay (New York: W.W. Norton Company, 2004), 2313.

6.   Henry Louis Gates Jr., *The Signifying Monkey: A Theory of African-American Literary Criticism* (New York: Oxford University Press, 1989), 196.

7. Morrison, "Unspeakable," 2313.

8. Charles Ruas, "Toni Morrison," in *Toni Morrison: Conversations*, ed. Carolyn C. Denard (Jackson, MS: University Press of Mississippi, 2008), 109.

9. Claudia Tate, "Toni Morrison," in *Conversations with Toni Morrison*, ed. Danille Taylor-Guthrie (Jackson, MS: University Press of Mississippi, 1994), 164.

10. Ruas, "Toni Morrison," 108-9.

11. Toni Morrison, *The Bluest Eye* (New York: Plume, 1970), 20 (hereafter cited in text).

12. Ann Hostetler, "Interview with Toni Morrison: 'The Art of Teaching,'" in *Toni Morrison: Conversations*, ed. Carolyn C. Denard (Jackson, MS: University Press of Mississippi, 2008), 199.

13. Hortense Spillers, "A Hateful Passion, A Lost Love: Three Women's Fiction," in *Black, White, and in Color: Essays on American Literature and Culture* (Chicago: University of Chicago Press, 2003), 93.

14. Robert Stepto, "Intimate Things in Place: A Conversation with Toni Morrison," in *Conversations with Toni Morrison*, ed. Danille Taylor-Guthrie (Jackson, MS: University Press of Mississippi, 1994), 12.

15. Toni Morrison, *Sula* (New York: Plume, 1973), 5 (hereafter cited in text).

16. Stepto, "Intimate Things," 13.

17. Barbara Smith, "Toward a Black Feminist Criticism," in *African American Literary Theory: A Reader*, ed. Winston Napier (New York: New York University Press, 2000), 142.

18. Audrey T. McCluskey, "A Conversation with Toni Morrison," in *Toni Morrison: Conversations*, ed. Carolyn C. Denard (Jackson, MS: University Press of Mississippi, 2008), 39.

19. Tate, "Toni Morrison," 157.

20. Smith, "Toward a Black Feminist Criticism," 138.

21. Audre Lorde, "Uses of the Erotic: The Erotic as Power," in *Sister Outsider: Essays and Speeches by Audre Lorde* (Freedom, CA: The Crossing Press, 1984), 55.

22. Black Creation Annual, "Conversation with Alice Childress and Toni Morrison," in *Conversations with Toni Morrison*, ed. Danille Taylor-Guthrie (Jackson, MS: University Press of Mississippi, 1994), 8.

23. Stepto, "Intimate Things," 14.

24. Mel Watkins, "Talk with Toni Morrison," in *Conversations with Toni Morrison*, ed. Danille Taylor-Guthrie (Jackson, MS: University Press of Mississippi, 1994), 46.

25.   Toni Morrison, *Song of Solomon* (New York: Plume, 1977), 4 (hereafter cited in text).

26.   Thomas LeClair, "'The Language Must Not Sweat': A Conversation with Toni Morrison," in *Conversations with Toni Morrison*, ed. Danille Taylor-Guthrie (Jackson, MS: University Press of Mississippi, 1994), 126.

Morrison arrives at the 2007 *Glamour* magazine "Women of the Year"
awards in New York. [AP Photo/Peter Kramer]

Toni Morrison poses with a copy of her book *Beloved* in New York City in 1987. [AP Photo/David Bookstaver]

Toni Morrison in 1993 at Princeton University in Princeton, N.J., where she was among 15 famous New Jerseyans selected as the first inductees to the New Jersey Hall of Fame. [AP Photo/Charles Rex Arbogast, File]

Morrison receives the Nobel Prize in literature from King Carl XVI Gustaf of Sweden, right, in the Concert Hall in Stockholm, Sweden, December 10, 1993. [AP Photo]

President Clinton embraces Toni Morrison after awarding her a National Humanities Medal in 2000. [AP Photo/Rick Bowmer]

Toni Morrison in her New York apartment in 1998. Above is a portrait of her painted when she was 23. [AP Photo/Jim Cooper]

Morrison, left, shares a moment with actors and activists Ossie Davis, center, and his wife Ruby Dee during a 70th birthday tribute for Morrison hosted by the Toni Morrison Society and Alfred A. Knopf, 2001. [AP Photo/Darla Khazei]

Morrison smiles as she is warmly received by the audience moments before giving the Radcliffe Inaugural Lecture on the Harvard University campus in 2001. The lecture helped commemorate the founding of the Radcliffe Institute for Advanced Study within Harvard University. [AP Photo/Steven Senne]

Chapter 5

CRITICAL RECOGNITION

With the publication of *Song of Solomon*, Morrison received widespread acclaim. In 1980, she was named to the National Council of the Arts by President Jimmy Carter, and a year later she was elected to the American Academy and Institute of Arts and Letters. Most importantly, she began thinking of herself as a writer. Following the widely anticipated publication of her fourth novel, *Tar Baby*, in 1981, she became the first black woman to appear on the cover of *Newsweek* since Zora Neale Hurston in 1943. The article named her "America's storyteller" and focused in particular on the impetus behind her most recent work.[1]

Tar Baby is set on an imaginary Caribbean Island and involves the love affair between Jadine, an educated black model, and Son, a handsome drifter. They meet at the estate of Valerian Street, a retired white millionaire, who is accompanied by his fragile wife, Margaret, and their black servants, Sydney and Ondine Childs. Although Jadine is the niece of Sydney and Ondine, she occupies a different social circle due to the patronage she receives from Valerian. Some critics found Morrison's exploration of social hierarchies to be overly didactic, while others described her portrayal of white characters as shallow and clichéd. Despite these mixed reviews, *Tar Baby* is marked by Morrison's signature lyrical style and her preoccupation with issues of community and identity.

Tar Baby is a departure from Morrison's previous work in a number of significant ways. It is the first of her novels in which white characters are central to the plot. Moreover, while her earlier works described a fairly cohesive African American community, *Tar Baby* abounds with individuals who, despite sharing certain identity traits, do not form a united group. For example, Sydney and Ondine do not even know the names of Gideon and Thérèse, the poor black workers who are hired to do especially laborious chores at Valerian's home, L'Arbe de la Croix. When Son enters the house, Sydney is outraged by his presence and is slow to accept him even when he becomes intimate with Jade. *Tar Baby* presents a series of couples who are each defined by specific racial and class categories and who consequently struggle to communicate effectively with one another.

To dramatize these various tensions, Morrison uses a considerable amount of dialogue, a narrative device employed only sparingly in her previous novels. Importantly, the conversations in *Tar Baby* are not extended monologues but instead involve fast banter that illustrate the hierarchies operating between the various characters. For example, in an opening exchange Valerian comments to Sydney about the Postum that Ondine prepares for him:

"And tell Ondine that half Postum and half coffee is revolting. Worse than Postum alone."

"Okay. Okay. She thought it would help."

"I know what she thought, but the help is worse than the problem."

"That might not be what the trouble is, you know."

"You are determined to make me have an ulcer. I don't have an ulcer. You have an ulcer. I have occasional irregularity."

"I *had* an ulcer. It's gone now and Postum helped it go."[2]

This dialogue reveals the intricate power dynamics between Valerian and his servants. Ondine attempts to deceive him with a half-measure of Postum in order to soothe his health problems. Valerian refuses to acknowledge the truth of his condition as well as the kindness of Ondine's gesture. Although Sydney bows to Valerian's newly asserted desire, he counters by stating that Postum helped him and could help Valerian as well. Their relationship is not a simplistic one of master and servant, but involves both tenderness and resistance on the side of Sydney and Ondine and nuanced forms of deception among them all.

A retired candy manufacturer, Valerian has moved to Isle des Chevaliers, where he has built a mansion to escape from the demands of work and social life. The island is named for a race of blind people descended from a group of slaves who lost their sight upon arriving at its beautiful shore. The slave ship sank and the cargo of human chattel and horses washed up on the island. Although some of the slaves were caught, those who were totally blind hid and are reputed to ride the horses through the hills. The myth of the blind horsemen highlights a form of knowledge based in intuition and nature that is alien to most of the novel's characters, especially Valerian, who insists that the island is named for French horsemen, not blind Africans. Nature plays a key role in this text, serving as a type of chorus that watches the events unfolding on the island. Morrison creates a world where clouds converse, butterflies become agitated, and water pushes like "the hand of an insistent woman" (4). This animated environment serves as a poignant reminder of all that existed before humans moved rivers to accommodate their desires and built elaborate homes atop the island's beauty. Like the ants and mildew that ceaselessly encroach upon the house, nature will persist and in the interim patiently watches the various dramas of its human inhabitants.

Of all the novel's characters, Valerian is the most detached from any meaningful relationship with the natural world. He idles in his greenhouse, where he grows northern flowers and listens to classical music. The greenhouse symbolizes Valerian's colonizing impulse, his attempt to bring order and civilization to the tropical jungle, while also illustrating his isolation from others. Valerian is especially distant from his much younger wife, Margaret, a former beauty queen who wants to return to their Philadelphia home. Margaret is slowly losing her ability to function in society; she forgets how to use dining implements and is often uncertain how to conduct herself socially. Her disorientation reflects her unease in Valerian's opulent house, a world entirely foreign to her lower-class origins. Because Valerian believes that Margaret's lapses are due to her alcoholism, he becomes enraged when she behaves incorrectly at the table. This critical misunderstanding under-scores years of failed communication that have defined their marriage and distanced both from Michael, their only son.

Tar Baby opens a few days before Christmas with Margaret con-vinced that Michael will finally join them at L'Arbe de la Croix. Instead of Michael, the household is visited by Son, a fugitive who has been hiding out in the storeroom and roaming the bedrooms by night. Margaret is terrified to find him in her closet, but while Sydney arms himself with a gun and marches Son to the dining room, Valerian invites the intruder to eat. Margaret, Sydney, and Ondine are out-raged, while Jadine is more reserved, deferring to the man who has financed her education. She soon finds herself irrevocably attracted to Son's beauty and confidence though they spar on critical cultural dif-ferences between them. He assumes that her success as a model has depended on her granting sexual favors. Most importantly, he calls her a white girl while she brands him a nigger.

These explosive exchanges illustrate the wide range of black iden-tity explored in the novel. Son is an easy symbol of authentic black identity given his comfort in the natural world, his strong connection to his family in Eloe, a small all-black town in Florida, and his disgust with Valerian's way of life. However, Jade represents another kind of blackness based in hybridity and social fluidity. *Tar Baby* is a love story between these two complex characters and explores how and if their deep cultural differences can be overcome. The tensions between Jadine and Son indicate that blackness is not a static essence but instead contains differences that are as intractable and complicated as differences between members of separate races.

The household explodes at Christmas dinner; Michael has once again failed to arrive, and the other expected guests are waylaid by bad weather on the mainland. Valerian insists that everyone gather for the meal Margaret promised to make herself but which Ondine had to fin-ish. The narrator notes that even prior to the dinner, "nobody was in his proper place" (194). With servant seated beside master and a law-less intruder in a stunning suit, the evening soon spins out of control. Sydney and Ondine are outraged to learn that Valerian has fired Gideon and Thérèse without first informing them. Son defends the poor island workers who were caught stealing the apples Valerian ordered specifically for the Christmas meal. In declaring that the kitchen is her domain, Ondine rebukes Margaret for her paltry attempt at cooking, stating, "She's no cook and she's no mother" (207). Valerian immediately fires Ondine, who then attacks Margaret, slapping her across the face. Ondine shocks everyone by accusing Margaret of physically torturing Michael when he was a boy. Margaret is powerless against the charge; she did stick needles into her son and burn him with cigarettes. Following this appalling revelation, the characters flee the scene, all except Valerian, who is too stunned to move. The dramatic dinner seems to validate Son's observation "that white folks and black folks should not sit down and eat together," although ultimately such exchanges are the only way for difficult truths to be aired (210).

Valerian eventually accepts blame for Margaret's actions, remembering how he used to find his son hidden beneath the sink, looking for something "soft" (74). He observed how erratic Margaret could be with Michael, but he chose not to intervene and thus must bear the consequences of his willed ignorance:

> He thought about innocence there in his greenhouse and knew that he was guilty of it because he had lived with a woman who had made something kneel down in him the first time he saw her, but about whom he knew nothing; had watched his son grow and talk but also about whom he knew nothing. And there was something so foul in that, something in the crime of innocence so revolting it paralyzed him. (242)

Valerian has refused the responsibility of knowledge; he knows no more than what is necessary to fulfill his own desires. Margaret, Michael, Sydney, and Ondine operate exclusively for his pleasure, not as people with needs of their own. Valerian is guilty of sequestering himself not only from truths too painful to acknowledge but also from an understanding of the true complexity of others. He knows nothing about Margaret, neither of her capacity for cruelty nor of her ability to be kind and generous. The narrator explains, "An innocent man is a sin before God. Inhuman and therefore unworthy" (243). By denying himself knowledge of others, Valerian has sacrificed his essential humanity and consequently condoned the abuse Margaret inflicted upon Michael.

Newly liberated by the public declaration of her crime, Margaret confronts Ondine to tell her, "You should have stopped me." Though Margaret conceded that it was not Ondine's "job" to do so, she explains, "I wish you had liked me enough to help me" (241). Ondine is also guilty of the abuse Michael suffered. Although she did not commit the torture, she allowed it to continue. Margaret understands Ondine's silence as emanating from the latter's desire to have them both fit caricatured images. "I could be the mean white lady and you could be the good colored one" (240). Ondine does not reply to Margaret's question, indicating both her guilt and her continued inability to speak freely with Margaret. By ceding to simplistic subject positions of evil versus good, Ondine has also failed to recognize Margaret's humanity and to address her own callous sanctioning of Michael's suffering.

At the conclusion of the novel, Valerian is reduced to infantile helplessness. His greenhouse is overrun with ants, and though he considers returning to Philadelphia, Sydney has decided that they will all stay at Isle des Chevaliers. As he drinks Valerian's wine, Sydney explains, "We'll give you the best of care. Just like we always done," but makes clear that all major decisions will be made by him and Ondine (287). Power between them has shifted dramatically as the servant becomes the master, and the master slips into a type of willed senility. Sydney's assertion of control is coupled with the return of the ants to Valerian's artificial sanctuary, suggesting that the civilized order of the white colonizer over nature has only been temporary.

The title of the novel comes from a black folk story, the most famous version of which is included in Joel Chandler Harris's *Nights with Uncle Remus* (1881). In the tale, the tar baby is a trap set by a white farmer to ensnare Brer Rabbit, who initially approaches the tar baby amicably. When the doll does not respond, Brer Rabbit becomes upset, kicking it for its lack of manners. Once he touches the tar baby he becomes stuck and is unable to return to his home in the briar patch. While Morrison directly references the story in the novel, her use of the term *tar baby* has an additional meaning as she explains:

"Tar Baby" is also a name, like nigger, that white people call black children, black girls, as I recall. . . . I found that there is a tar lady in African mythology. . . . At one time, a tar pit was a holy place.

. . . [Tar] held together things like Moses's little boat and the pyr-
amids. For me, the tar baby came to mean the black woman who
could hold things together. The story was a point of departure to
history and prophecy.[3]

Jadine operates as the tar baby of Morrison's novel, but in multiple
ways. She entraps Son through her sexual allure, but she is also the
character in the novel who is best able to bring people together. She
accomplishes this not through love like Pilate or by creating a physical home like Eva; instead Jade is distinguished by her ability to converse with people across race and class lines. She occupies a unique
position in that as the niece of Ondine and Sydney, she does not share
their subservient position to Valerian and Margaret. Her French education and career as a model link her to the sophistication and leisure
enjoyed by the Streets. When visiting Isle des Chevaliers, Jade stays in
a guestroom in the main house and dines with Valerian and Margaret
while her uncle waits upon them all. However, she is also welcome to
gossip in the kitchen with her aunt, a privilege denied to Margaret.
Jade is able to move through these various spaces because of her outsider status; she is an orphan, and her impressive education and experiences abroad separate her from other African Americans. In reaching
out to white characters, Jade offers the hope of meaningful interracial
dialogue.

While Jade's fluid identity enables her to speak with a wide variety
of people, it also plagues her with a sense of inauthenticity. While in a
Paris grocery store, she encounters a tall, dark-skinned woman in a
bright yellow dress buying three eggs. Jadine is struck by the woman's
"confidence of transcendent beauty," a "woman's woman . . . that
unphotographable beauty." In a devastating moment, the woman
"turned those eyes too beautiful for eyelashes on Jadine and, with a
small parting of her lips, shot an arrow of saliva" (46). For Jadine, the
woman in the yellow dress is a figure of authentic, confident black
identity. This is the very issue that leads Son to conclude that Jadine
has lost her "ancient properties" because she has no meaningful link to
a black community (305).

By contrast, Son is portrayed as fundamentally attuned to his
African American roots. Although he has been apart from his family

and hometown since accidentally killing his wife, he longs to return to Eloe and make a life there with Jade. The two initially escape the upheaval at Isle des Chevaliers by traveling to New York, but Son becomes anxious in a city where he cannot find the carefree inno-cence of childhood; "There were short people and people under twelve years of age, but they had no child's vulnerability, no unstuck laughter" (215). Son insists upon taking Jadine to Eloe, which he envisions as a place "presided over by wide black women in snowy dresses and was ever dry, green and quiet" (168). Jade, however, finds the town stifling and backward, full of people with antiquated ideas and suspicious questions.

After Son sneaks into her room one night, Jade is awakened by the sense that she is surrounded by all the women she has ever known, including her mother and the woman in the yellow dress. As they watch her, they each bare their breasts, and though Jadine proclaims, "I have breasts too," they "just held their own higher and pushed their own farther out" (259). The scene emphasizes Jadine's insecurities with her own identity; with no desire for children and no rooted com-munity of her own, is she a real woman? The women flaunt their breasts, symbols of sustenance and life, challenging Jadine to prove her womanhood. Ondine later explains to her niece that "a girl has got to be a daughter first . . . And if she never learns how to be a daughter, she can't never learn how to be a woman" (281). As an orphan who was largely educated in boarding schools, Jadine never developed sta-ble relationships with others and therefore she focuses far more on immediate circumstances and where she plans to go next. As the nar-rator explains of Jadine and Son, "One had a past, the other a future and each one bore the culture to save the race in his hands" (269). This fundamental conflict between Son's romanticized vision of the past and Jade's desire to create a wholly new life ultimately splits the two apart.

Jade returns to Paris convinced that "She *was* the safety she longed for" while Son futilely chases her back to Isle des Chevaliers (290). There he encounters Gideon, who tells him that Jade is gone. Unde-terred, Son insists on returning to L'Arbe de la Croix and Thérèse agrees to ferry him there. She takes him to the back of the island, telling Son that he now has a choice and he can join the blind horsemen. As Son crawls toward the island, the "mist lifted and the trees stepped back a bit as if to make the way easier for a certain kind of man." Although Morrison does not definitively state that Son joins the horsemen, the way in which the trees welcome him ashore suggests that he is at last united with nature. Like the rabbit who escapes the tar baby, Son returns to his briar batch, running "Lickety-split" (306).

Morrison continued to explore relationships across racial divisions in her next literary work, her only short story. "Recitatif," which explores the relationship between two girls, one black and one white, appeared in *Confirmation: An Anthology of African American Women* (1983), edited by Amiri Baraka and his wife, Amina. In the introduction, Baraka explains that his purpose in compiling the collection "is to draw attention to the existence and excellence of black women writers."[4] Concerned by the dominance of texts by white, bourgeois men in general conceptions of American letters, Baraka aims to highlight "the injustice of black women's low profile in the world of literature—and at the same time to do something about it" by letting "black women speak for themselves."[5] Baraka notes how the stories and poems collected in *Confirmation* present a multidimensional world that describes routine oppression and exploitation but also voices a legacy of beauty and dynamic creativity.

The title of Morrison's contribution to *Confirmation*, "Recitatif," refers to a musical term that describes a type of vocal writing that most often mimics dramatic speech. Repetition and mimicry are both key themes to the story, which explores how successive returns to a specific childhood memory are influenced by immediate circumstances; our understanding of the past is always an imitation of the present. "Recitatif" is narrated by Twyla, a grown woman who reflects upon her troubled childhood and her uneven lifelong relationship with Roberta. The two meet as young girls at a shelter where they have both been abandoned by their mothers. In the opening line, Twyla explains, "My mother danced all night and Roberta's was sick." Despite being initially reluctant to room with Roberta, "a girl from a whole other race," Twyla quickly comes to appreciate "the way she understood things so fast."[6] Twyla does not need to explain the reason she has been left at the shelter, and it is precisely through their mutual abandonment that their friendship flourishes. Although the two are described as "salt and pepper," Morrison refuses to specify the race of the two girls. Only tangential references are made to race. Twyla, for example, mentions that those of Roberta's race "never washed their hair and they smelled funny" (445). When they encounter one another as young women, Roberta is on her way to see Jimi Hendrix. These clues to racial identity are elusive since lack of hygiene has been attributed to both blacks and whites, and Hendrix, while black, generated a largely white following.

To assign specific racial identities to Twyla and Roberta depends on the reader's own stereotypes. To interpret Twyla as black suggests that African Americans may be more inclined to a lower-class lifestyle as she waitresses for a living while Roberta eventually marries a rich widower. However, the text also supports a reading of Roberta as black; Roberta arrives at the shelter illiterate, and later Twyla describes her hair as "so big and wild I could hardly see her face"—might that be a reference to an afro (451)? The racial ambiguity of Twyla and Roberta can be infuriating for first-time readers of "Recitatif," but ultimately the search for racial clues emphasizes the reader's own need for such identification. Because race cannot be definitively assigned to the characters, Morrison asks us to consider why racial categorization even matters. Would we know these characters better if we knew who was black and who was white? What safety or comfort does racial identity provide readers?

As girls, Twyla and Roberta are bound by a common experience that is independent of race. Abandoned by their mothers and bullied by the older girls at the shelter, the two form an abiding bond. Later racial difference intrudes upon them as they take opposite sides in a school busing protest. However, their key conflict arises in how they each remember an older kitchen worker at the shelter, a mute woman named Maggie whom Twyla describes as "old and sandy-colored" (447). One afternoon Maggie falls as she walks home and the older girls laugh while Twyla and Roberta silently watch. Later, Roberta tells Twyla that Maggie was knocked down and attacked by the older girls. In a subsequent encounter Roberta claims that they were both involved, that they too kicked Maggie, whom she identifies as black. Twyla is bewildered by the accusation and uncertain of Maggie's racial identity. Referring to the mute woman, she reflects:

She wasn't pitch-black, I knew, or I would have remembered that. What I remember was the kiddie hat, and the semicircle legs. I tried to reassure myself about the race thing for a long time until it dawned on me that the truth was already there, and Roberta knew it. I didn't kick her . . . but I sure wanted to. We watched and never tried to help her and never called for help. (462)

Maggie's race is secondary to the desire of the two friends to hurt the older woman. She becomes the focus of their frustrated rage, a representation of their powerless mothers who cannot protect themselves much less their daughters. In their last meeting, Roberta tells Twyla that she is in fact not certain that Maggie was black and that she lied about their involvement in the attack. However, the final line of the story, "What the hell happened to Maggie?" suggests that the two may only be constructing their own more comfortable version of events; ultimately, the truth remains elusive (464). Their shared guilt indicates that Maggie's indeterminate racial identity is far less critical than how and why they developed a need to dominate her. This urge to assert power over another does not depend on racial difference even if race is often used to justify such aggression.

The same year that "Recitatif" was published, Morrison left Random House and began teaching creative writing at the State University of New York in Albany as the Albert Schweitzer Professor of the Humanities. During this time, she began composing the unpublished play *Dreaming Emmett*, which was commissioned by the New York State Writers Institute at SUNY-Albany and directed by Gilbert Moses. The idea behind the play came to Morrison years earlier, but with the commission provided by the Writers Institute, she took the opportunity to complete her only dramatic work. In describing the genesis of *Dreaming Emmett*, Morrison emphasizes that it emerged "not as a novel, or an essay, but as a play. I wanted to see a collision of three or four levels of time through the eyes of one person who could come back to life and seek vengeance. Emmett Till became that person."[7] Till was a fourteen-year-old boy from Chicago who while visiting family in Mississippi was brutally beaten and murdered in 1955. The day before his murder he had whistled at a white woman. The men who were charged with the crime were acquitted though they later confessed. The infamous case highlighted the rampant injustice against African Americans in the South and galvanized the nascent civil rights movement.

In her play, Morrison presents an anonymous boy who returns thirty years after his death in order to understand the circumstances of his murder. The nonlinear scenes include members of his family, friends, and the men who killed him. Although they initially appear as figures conjured by his will and imagination, he is unable to control them and they proceed to tell their own version of events. History merges with dream as Till speaks from the dead and tries to understand the meaning behind his brutal death. Although Morrison focuses on a specific crime that occurred in 1955, the play reflects her concern with contemporary issues facing black men. As she explained in an interview immediately prior to the premier of *Dreaming Emmett* at the Market Theatre in Albany:

> There are these young black men getting shot all over the country today, not because they were stealing but because they're black. And no one remembers how any of them looked. No one even remembers the facts of each case.[8]

Hostility and suspicion continue to plague the lives of African American men and by exploring the circumstances of Till's death, Morrison spotlights an important contemporary issue facing the black community.

Morrison found the experience of working in the theater to be engaging though quite different from the process of writing novels. She reflected,

> The play is both more and less. It's less in the setting of a mood and in manipulating readers. In the novel one has control of everything. Giving that up in a play is not pleasant for me. But on the other hand, there is a thing that happens on the stage. After giving up control, you see the manifestation of the work through somebody else's mind . . . When you hear the actresses and actors read they give new meanings to the lines and so the texture of the play changes. But in a novel, I only hear it one way, through my voice.[9]

Although Morrison has not returned to drama, she has since experimented with musical scores and poetry.

Morrison continued to explore voices beyond the grave in her internationally acclaimed bestseller *Beloved*. Set in Reconstruction-era Ohio, *Beloved* tells the story of Sethe, an escaped slave woman who murders her daughter rather than return to a life of bondage. Morrison describes Sethe's struggle to keep her slave memories from consciousness along with her need to confront the ghosts of her past. Sethe's repression is unsettled by the arrival of Paul D, a man she knew in slavery, and Beloved, a troubling stranger who doesn't seem to know who she is and who may in fact be the daughter Sethe killed so that she would not be returned to slavery. In this powerful novel, Morrison describes the dehumanizing effects of slavery and the complexities of maternal love. *Beloved* is often considered Morrison's masterpiece, but it has generated significant debate concerning its literary merit and its presentation of past atrocities.

Although most critics praised the novel for its soaring prose, innovative narration, and rich characterizations, controversy erupted after it failed to win the National Book Award and the National Book Critics Circle Award. In response, forty-eight prominent African American writers and intellectuals, including Maya Angelou, Alice Walker, and John Wideman, published a letter in the *New York Times* decrying this oversight: "Alive, we write this testament of thanks to you, dear Toni: alive, beloved and persevering, magical. . . . For all America, for all of American letters, you have advanced the moral and artistic standards by which we must measure the daring and the love of our national imagination and our collective intelligence as a people."[10] Later that year, *Beloved* was awarded the Pulitzer Prize, and it continues to be hailed as a major contribution to American literature.

The letter of support was unprecedented and wholly unexpected for Morrison, who later commented on the influence it may have had on the Pulitzer committee:

> That was a kind of blessing for me—to know that irrespective of the formal recognition that is available to a writer, that they appreciated the worth of my work to them. They redeemed me, but I am certain they played no significant role in the judgment. If anything, it was in the teeth of speculation and gossip that the Pulitzer committee was forced to operate. They apparently resisted it.[11]

Ralph Ellison was notably absent from the signers of the letter to the *New York Times* though he was pleased that *Beloved* ultimately won the Pulitzer: "Good for Toni. I was pretty annoyed with some of the stuff that's been boiling about her not getting recognition. Toni doesn't need that kind of support even though it was well-intentioned. She can compete with the best writers anywhere. Sometimes it's a matter of luck and who is on the committee. Look how long Hemingway and Faulkner had to wait to get their just awards."[12] Though Ellison also noted that he never won a Pulitzer, *Beloved* would share a special honor with *Invisible Man*. In 2006, it was named the Best Work of American Fiction of the Last 25 Years by the *New York Times*; the previous winner of such a title was *Invisible Man*.

Morrison initially conceived *Beloved* as a three-volume work, and when she handed her working manuscript to her editor, Robert Gottlieb, she was convinced that it was a failure. He read the work and recognized it as a coherent whole. Morrison added the page-and-a-half conclusion, and the manuscript was ready for publication. The book is loosely based on the story of Margaret Garner, which Morrison discovered when she was researching *The Black Book*. A slave woman who escaped to the North with her four young children, Garner chose to kill them rather than allow herself and her family to return to bondage. Following her capture, Garner was notably serene in interviews, simply stating, "I will not let those children live how I have lived." Her mother-in-law witnessed the event and according to Morrison said, "I neither encouraged her nor discouraged her."[13] Morrison limited her study of Garner's life history so that she would be free to envision the novel on her own and explore the central questions that Garner's story raised for her. Morrison became fascinated with the nature of maternal love and the lengths that mothers will go to protect their children. As she pondered Garner's choice, she concluded that only the dead child had the right to question her mother's astounding decision.

The character Beloved, a confused young woman who appears at Sethe's house on 124 Bluestone Road, is most often read as the reincarnation of the child Sethe murdered upon seeing that slavecatchers had tracked her to her mother-in-law's house in the free state of Ohio. However, the text supports additional readings of Beloved. Her memories of bondage aboard a ship suggest that she survived the Middle

Passage, the forcible journey of Africans to the New World. Alternatively, she may have been kept as a sexual slave at a neighboring plantation. These varied readings of Beloved also highlight the many ways that critics have approached the novel. It portrays complex dynamics that reflect insights derived from psychoanalysis, trauma theory, critical race theory, and black feminist thought. Despite these multiple ways of interpreting both the text and the figure of Beloved, the ultimate effect that the latter has upon Sethe is to unearth the older woman's repressed memories of slavery. The book opens in 1873, a decade after the end of the Civil War. Following the death of her mother-in-law, Baby Suggs, Sethe lives alone with her youngest daughter, Denver. The two are severely isolated from the local black community because of Sethe's scandalous history. They are also plagued by a ghost that haunts their house and which is responsible for scaring off Sethe's two older sons.

The first chapter describes the arrival of Paul D, one of five men who worked the Kentucky plantation, Sweet Home, which Sethe joined when she was fourteen. She was purchased in order to replace Baby Suggs, whom Halle, her son, bought by working five years of Sundays. The men wait for Sethe to choose a husband, and she decides upon Halle; together they have four children. At the start of the novel eighteen years have passed since Paul D and Sethe last saw each other at Sweet Home, and as they piece together the past, they come to a deeper understanding of how Sethe and Halle's plan for escape failed while also releasing the memories that have long haunted them. In their first encounter, Sethe tells Paul D how schoolteacher, the man who took over Sweet Home after Mr. Garner, the farm's mild owner, dies and his nephews beat her and stole her milk. Obsessed with cataloging the bestial characteristics of slaves, schoolteacher allows his nephews to suckle Sethe and whip her despite the fact that she was six months pregnant with Denver. Paul D later tells her that Halle had been trapped in the loft while this violation occurred, and together they conclude that this is the reason Halle did not meet Sethe as planned. She made the journey alone, pregnant and dripping milk for the baby daughter that awaited her at 124 Bluestone. Paul D also intended to run away but was caught by schoolteacher and manacled with a bit, an antebellum torture device.

With Paul D, Sethe is at last safe to remember the painful past. She tentatively ponders the possibility of their love: "Trust things and remember things because the last of the Sweet Home men was there to catch her if she sank?"[14] Sethe has shared only small pieces of her life story with Denver because she is wary of what she calls her "rememory," images from her past that stay "out there, in the world. . . . Right in the place where it happened" (37). For this reason, she shelters Denver from the past and from specific places that harbor memories too painful to recall. Isolated from others and uncertain of her mother's history, Denver becomes an anxious, secretive child. She relishes the ghost as her sole companion and tentatively goads her mother to repeat the story of how she was born.

Denver's birth is told in overlapping installments, in part as Sethe's recollection and also through Denver, whose development depends on her ability to understand and share her mother's history. Alone in the woods and badly hurt from the whipping she received by schoolteacher and his nephews, Sethe encounters Amy Denver, a white indentured servant making her own escape to Boston. Amy leads Sethe to a lean-to where she massages the slavewoman's feet and describes her bloodied back as a chokecherry tree with "Tiny little cherry blossoms" (79). Sethe repeats this description to Paul D when he first arrives, emphasizing how the painful past can be transformed and ultimately yield new life. As Amy sings to Sethe and tells her about the carmine velvet she intends to buy in Boston, these "two throw-away people, two lawless outlaws" develop an unlikely alliance (84). During their attempt to cross the Ohio River in a broken canoe, Sethe gives birth to Denver, naming her after the white girl. In a novel filled with shocking acts of brutality committed by whites against blacks, the scenes involving Amy and Sethe offer the hope of meaningful interracial cooperation. Moreover, Amy's status as an indentured servant who has inherited her social position because of her mother's death indicates that blacks were not the only victims of bondage in the antebellum South.

With Paul D, Sethe ventures into other aspects of her repressed past, but this release upsets the ghost dwelling in the house. As soon as Sethe tells how her milk was stolen, the house convulses with rage. Paul D violently exorcises the ghost, but days later Beloved, dressed in black silk and with no lines on her hands, appears at their doorstep. Upon seeing her, Sethe is overcome by an urgent need to urinate, suggesting that her water is newly broken by the arrival of this stranger. Unable to describe who she is or where she has come from, Beloved drinks glass after glass of water and then collapses on Baby Suggs's bed. Denver protectively cares for her until she is strong enough to eat the sweet foods that she craves. Paul D is wary of the mysterious woman, who urges Sethe to "Tell me your diamonds" (58). Sethe thus recalls how Mrs. Garner gave her crystal earrings after she decided to marry Halle. Though Sethe wanted a wedding, Mrs. Garner was content to mark Sethe's decision by simply having her move her pallet and night bucket next to his. So immersed in her memory, Sethe does not wonder how Beloved knew to ask about the diamonds.

Beloved develops a possessive attachment toward Sethe, much like an infant demanding maternal attention. She becomes hostile toward Paul D, who finds himself so unsettled in the house that he can no longer sleep inside. He moves out to the storeroom where Beloved appears to him at night, demanding that he "touch me on the inside part and call me my name" (116). Although Paul D orders her away, he is unable to resist her advances. As they have sex, Beloved affirms that her focus is entirely on Sethe, stating, "She don't love me like I love her. I don't love nobody but her" (116). By seducing Paul D, Beloved hopes to destroy the bond between him and Sethe. His presence threatens the full attention she demands of Sethe.

Paul D eventually leaves 124 Bluestone but not because of his coupling with Beloved. Instead he learns from Stamp Paid, the man who initially found Sethe and Denver on the river after Amy left, that Sethe tried to kill her children when schoolteacher tracked her to Ohio. Paul D confronts Sethe with this information, and she tells him of the transformation that occurred in her when she first realized she was free:

> I was big, Paul D, and deep and wide and when I stretched out my arms all my children could get in between. I was that wide. Look like I loved em more after I got here. Or maybe I couldn't love em proper in Kentucky because they wasn't mine to love. But when I got here, when I jumped down off that wagon—there wasn't

nobody in the world I couldn't love if I wanted to. You know what I mean? (162)

Sethe here describes how freedom from bondage is fundamentally based in the freedom to love. Slavery prevented individuals from trusting in personal relationships because at any time family members could be sold. Paul D has also struggled with this conflict; he learns to love in small amounts, focusing on objects like "grass blades, salamanders, spiders" because "anything bigger wouldn't do. A woman, a child, a brother—a big love like that would split you wide open" (162). By focusing on the emotional hardships imposed by slavery, Morrison emphasizes violence that is not simply physical but which has lasting consequences on how individuals dare to relate to one another.

Unlike Ella, a former slave woman who was kept for the sexual perversions of a father and son and who proclaims, "Don't love nothing," Sethe audaciously loves her children. She refuses to have her children subjected to the violence and debasement that she suffered under schoolteacher. Referring to her decision to murder her children, she declares, "I took and put my babies where they'd be safe." The narrator further explains, "The best thing she was, was her children. Whites might dirty her all right, but not her best thing, her beautiful, magical best thing—the part of her that was clean" (251). Frightened and appalled by Sethe's action, Paul D calls her love "too thick," to which she replies, "Love is or it ain't. Thin love ain't love at all" (164).

Despite this critical difference in how Sethe and Paul D view love, the final schism between them occurs when he states, "You got two feet, Sethe, not four" (165). Paul D's comment echoes with the dehumanizing efforts of schoolteacher to catalog the bestial characteristics of the Sweet Home slaves. By calling her choice the act of an animal, Paul D fails to understand its fundamentally human motivation. Sethe's violence is born of love, not animal aggression. Only later will he consider that his comment may be derived from his own shame, the outrage he felt looking at a rooster, free to strut through the yard, while he wore the bit. The pride underlying Sethe's act frightens him, and he leaves her alone with Denver and Beloved.

Later, while listening to Beloved hum a tune that she created for her children, Sethe comes to believe that Beloved is her daughter returned from the dead. The realization thrills her, entirely negating the hurt left by Paul D's absence. She believes that at last her world is complete and concludes, "I won't never let her go. I'll explain to her, even though I don't have to. Why I did it" (200). Sethe recalls the full circumstances that prompted her to leave Sweet Home, remembering how she struggled to care for her children without someone to advise her, how she tended to the dying Mrs. Garner and made the ink that schoolteacher used to write up the value of each of the slaves as well as their animal qualities.

However, in the telling of these stories, Sethe becomes consumed by the past, losing all connection to the outside world. She loses her job and spends all of her time amusing her two daughters with toys, ribbons, and rich foods. Initially Denver is allowed to participate in the games that Sethe and Beloved play together, but she is soon ostracized by the consuming love between her sister and mother. Beloved becomes increasingly demanding and anxiously imitates Sethe so that "it was difficult for Denver to tell who was who" (241). This troubling merger of identity signals the danger of how traumatic memories can overwhelm the present and make functional daily life impossible. Beloved needles Sethe about the past so that the older woman must repeat how she loved Beloved, how she never wanted to leave her, and how she killed her only to save her from a worse fate. Even when Beloved is calm, Sethe goads her with additional details so that the narrative of her slave experience becomes the only language of the household.

Watching her mother literally shrink before the growing Beloved, who is pregnant with Paul D's child, Denver, "Her father's daughter after all," decides to leave 124 Bluestone in search of work and help (252). As she exits the yard that she has not ventured from in a dozen years, Denver remembers the courage and strength of Baby Suggs, demonstrating how memory can be constructive when it is not mired in obsessive repetition. Denver returns to the home of Lady Jones, the former schoolteacher who once taught classes to local black children. She stopped attending classes when a boy asked her about Sethe's stay in prison. Lady Jones welcomes Denver, and though she doesn't have work for Denver, she sends her home with rice and eggs. Soon after, Denver discovers plates of food left at the edge of the yard. As news of Denver's troubles emerges within the community and the local women come to understand that a reincarnation of Sethe's dead daughter is now living in the house, Ella decides that rescue is necessary. Ella scorned Sethe for the murder of her daughter, but she "didn't like the idea of past errors taking possession of the present" and thus organizes a group of women to restore order (257).

The return of the black community as an active force in Sethe's life marks a key development from her previous history. When school-teacher and his posse, described as "the four horsemen," like the har-bingers of the Apocalypse, first arrive to return Sethe and her children to Sweet Home, no one comes to warn the residents of 124 Bluestone (148). This significant failure is due to what Stamp Paid identifies as a type of "meanness" emanating from disapproval at the pride Baby Suggs and Sethe display in the aftermath of the latter's escape from slavery (157). The day before schoolteacher arrives, Baby Suggs hosts a party, an impromptu gathering inspired by Stamp Paid, who delivers two buckets of blackberries to her doorstep. The next morning, Baby is struck by a sense of "free-floating repulsion" and realizes that her "friends and neighbors were angry at her because she had overstepped, given too much, offended them by excess" (138). Without someone to alert them of schoolteacher's arrival, the slavecatchers easily find Sethe, who only has time to gather her children in the woodshed.

As Ella and the local women approach the house, "the first thing they saw was not Denver sitting on the steps, but themselves" (258). By recognizing an image of themselves in Denver, the women trans-form their confrontation with Beloved into one involving their own pasts and the need to safeguard the present from former trauma. Sethe is indifferent to their arrival because it coincides with that of Mr. Bod-win, the owner of 124 Bluestone, who has agreed to hire Denver. His horse and hat remind Sethe of schoolteacher and she rushes forth, ice pick in hand, to slay the man who would return her daughter to slav-ery. However, the women prevent her from reaching Mr. Bodwin, who is too confused by the spectacle to understand Sethe's intentions. Beloved watches as Sethe is absorbed into the group of women, form-ing a "hill of black people, falling" (262). She then disappears, exor-cised by the community who banish her back to the past.

After learning of Beloved's demise from Stamp Paid, Paul D returns to 124 Bluestone. He finds Sethe in bed and realizes that despite knowing his deepest shames, "Only this woman Sethe could have left him with his manhood like that." While he may have questioned his own humanity as well as hers, she always knew his worth. Sethe, however, is still distraught over the disappearance of Beloved, who she believed was her "best thing." Paul D counters, "You your best, Sethe. You are" to which she responds, "Me? Me?" Although she remains unconvinced of Paul D's assertion, her question suggests the possibility that she will eventually understand her own self-worth. Paul D returns "to put his story next to hers," explaining to Sethe that "we got more yesterday than anybody. We need some kind of tomorrow" (273). Together they will know the past without allowing it to govern their present.

The concluding pages of the novel, however, present a more ambiguous approach toward traumatic history. The text repeats three times, "This is not a story to pass on" (275). Depending on how one reads the verb *pass*, this statement can be read both as an injunction to forget the past and as an injunction to preserve it (do not dismiss this story). The contradictory interpretations of this line indicate both the dangers and the necessity of remembering. While the characters who knew Beloved choose to forget her because "Remembering seemed unwise," the text stands as a critical testament to the importance of preserving a meaningful understanding of the past (274). Sethe, Paul D, and Denver may release their memories of Beloved, but readers are enjoined to embrace her story.

The same year of *Beloved*'s publication, writer and poet Nikki Giovanni offered a class at Virginia Tech entirely focused on Morrison's work, the first of its kind but now a common course listing across university campuses both here and abroad. The following year, the first critical book devoted exclusively to Morrison, Terry Otten's *The Crime of Innocence in the Fiction of Toni Morrison* (1989), was published. It has since been followed by dozens of academic books that examine Morrison's works from a range of perspectives, historical contexts, and primary themes.

In 1988, Morrison left SUNY-Albany to become the Jeanette K. Watson Distinguished Professor at Syracuse University. However, a year later, Dr. Ruth Simmons, a dean at Princeton University who in 2001 became the first African American president of an Ivy League university when she accepted the position at Brown, invited Morrison to consider working at Princeton. Simmons asked for her resume, but

Morrison was dismayed at having to abide by conventional channels of employment. She refused to submit her resume while Princeton refused to hire a candidate without a printed history of her education and achievements. Simmons decided to take the matter into her own hands, writing up Morrison's resume and submitting the document herself. In short order, Morrison was named the Robert F. Goheen Professorship of the Humanities at Princeton University, becoming the first black woman to hold an endowed chair at an Ivy League school. It would be more than a decade before Morrison learned that Simmons was responsible for writing and submitting her resume; similarly Princeton officials had no idea about Simmons's intervention. Morrison's appointment was part of a major effort at Princeton to develop its African American Studies program. She was joined by such prominent black intellectuals as Cornel West and Arnold Rampersand.

Most of the teaching Morrison undertook at Princeton was in creative writing. Here she revisited her role as an editor, helping students to understand and develop the strengths of their work while also suggesting areas for new possibilities. These classes tended to be small, no more than five or six students whom Morrison met with individually four times throughout the semester. She believes that "analysis and passion" are the two most important aspects of teaching.[15] Her ultimate pedagogical goal is to encourage students to develop a critical language. Morrison often brings unedited manuscripts that she has bought through Random House to class and asks students to evaluate the work. However, instead of returning these comments to the author, she has students make their own changes to the manuscript, forcing them to respond to their own criticisms. Morrison finds that it is difficult to teach and write at the same time because while the former involves analytical critique and the breaking down of meaning, the latter requires the construction of ideas, images, and characters. Although she appreciates the rewards of teaching, she finds the greatest fulfillment in her writing. Nonetheless, while teaching creative writing and working with the African American, American, and Women's Studies departments at Princeton, Morrison began work on her sixth novel, *Jazz*.

Morrison conceived *Beloved* as the first part of a trilogy that would examine various aspects of love. *Jazz* is the second novel in this series, and like its predecessor it is derived from a historical artifact. Morrison drew her inspiration for *Jazz* from a photograph she saw in *The Harlem Book of the Dead* (1978), a collection of photographs taken by James Van Der Zee in the 1920s. The photographs consist primarily of dead black New Yorkers and reflect the practice of dressing deceased loved ones in fashionable attire. Morrison was especially taken by a photograph of the corpse of an eighteen-year-old girl. The adjoining caption indicates that the girl was shot while dancing at a rent party. She was murdered by a jealous ex-boyfriend, but when her friends asked who shot her, she refused to tell them. She loved him enough to let him go free, promising her friends that she would reveal his identity tomorrow; instead she died.

Jazz is set in what has become known as the Jazz Age, a dynamic historical time period in which the Harlem Renaissance emerged as a powerful literary and artistic movement and African Americans enjoyed new freedoms and opportunities. Following "The War to End All Wars" in 1918, over one million blacks moved from the South to the North, a massive exodus known as the Great Migration. African Americans fled the segregation and violence of the South as well as a devastating infestation of boll weevil to take part in the industrial expansion of the North. The end of World War I had created a new demand for labor as millions of men served in the armed forces and immigration decreased. The Great Migration created the first large, urban communities in the North, and Harlem became the center of black artistic and intellectual development. Writer and social critic Alain Locke's call for a "New Negro" movement galvanized poets, musicians, and artists to develop unique forms of black expression.

The most technically ambitious of Morrison's books, *Jazz* does not focus on the luminaries of the Harlem Renaissance, writers like Langston Hughes, Claude McKay, and Zora Neale Hurston, but instead examines the lives of everyday people who experienced both the thrills and the dangers of life in New York. Referred to only as "the City," New York plays a key role in the text. The City wields a powerful seductive influence with its bold promises of freedom and possibility; it "makes people think they can do what they want and get away with it."[16] However, such reinventions prove disorienting and destabilizing for the characters of *Jazz* including the text's unnamed and unreliable narrator. While demanding a collaborative storytelling relationship with the audience, this enigmatic voice describes the violent love triangle between Violet and Joe Trace and a haughty teenager named Dorcas. The narrator details Joe's love affair with Dorcas and his subsequent murder of the young girl against the thrilling sense of possibility that New York offered blacks following the Great Migration. Although *Jazz* received mixed reviews, it confirmed Morrison's commitment to taking stylistic risks in her work and demonstrated her belief in the dynamic nature of storytelling.

Morrison tells the entire plot of *Jazz* in the opening paragraph, thus encouraging readers to focus on the mode of narration, not just the subject of the story:

> Sth, I know that woman. She used to live with a flock of birds on Lenox Avenue. Know her husband, too. He fell for an eighteen-year-old girl with one of those deepdown, spooky loves that made him so sad and happy he shot her just to keep the feeling going. When the woman, her name is Violet, went to the funeral to see the girl and to cut her dead face they threw her to the floor and out of the church. (3)

Throughout *Jazz*, Morrison describes the same event in multiple ways, using various vantage points and narrative perspectives. By establishing the novel's core events, Morrison is free to return to the story, essentially "riffing" on the story much like a group of jazz musicians improvising upon a basic melody. Moreover, the contradiction of emotions apparent in Joe's love for Dorcas, a love that "made him so sad and happy," aligns the text with a distinctly blues aesthetic. As Ralph Ellison noted, "The blues is an art of ambiguity, an assertion of the irrepressibly human over all circumstance whether created by others or by one's own human failings."[17] The relationships between Joe, Violet, and Dorcas showcase complex interactions and highlight the contradictory impulses of human emotion as in the simultaneous desire to kill and protect the beloved. However, confronting this paradox also leads to the possibility of forgiveness and the survival of love beyond its destructive consequences.

Both Joe and Violet are from the South and they arrive in Harlem, dancing on the vibrations of a train, with the hope of creating a new life, one that leaves the past firmly behind. However, as in *Beloved*, escape from traumatic history proves to be illusory and destructive. Violet's mother, Rose Dear, unable to face the prolonged absences of her traveling husband and the loss of the family farm, jumped into a well. She left Violet and her four siblings, all "children of suicides" who "are hard to please and quick to believe no one loves them because they are not really here" (4). Violet struggles to affirm her sense of self in the aftermath of her mother's death and the arrival of her grand-mother True Belle, who raises the orphaned children and infects their imaginations with stories of Golden Gray, the mulatto son of Vera Louise, True Belle's former master.

The image of a golden-haired boy, beloved and coddled by True Belle and Vera Louise, haunts Violet and becomes the primary figure of her childhood memory. His beauty and ambiguous social position as both mixed-race and fatherless leaves Violet with a legacy premised upon a sense of superficial self reinvention. Consequently, Violet resolves never to have children, and after she is ordered by True Belle to harvest the bumper cotton crop in the town of Palestine, she never returns home. There she meets Joe Trace, who one night falls out of a tree where he had been sleeping. Violet chooses Joe and soon after they marry, living together in the rural South before then moving to Baltimore and finally the City.

Joe also has a traumatic childhood history, and unbeknownst to both him and Violet, their two family stories are intertwined. Upon learning that he is the son of a black man, the former slave of his mother's family, Golden Gray sets out to meet his father, Henry Lestory. On the way, he encounters a pregnant, naked black woman who, in her rush to flee, runs headlong into a tree branch and is knocked unconscious. Golden Gray wraps her in his coat and carries her to Lestory's cabin. When Lestory, who is locally known as Hunters Hunter due to his consummate skills in the woods, returns, the preg-nant woman awakens and bites him on the cheek. Lestory names her "Wild," but she might easily be understood as another incarnation of Beloved, who vanishes pregnant and naked at the end of Morrison's previous novel. After giving birth to Joe, Wild returns to the woods, only to be spotted sporadically. Although Joe is taken in by a loving family, he is traumatized by the absence of his parents. When he asks his adopted mother about them, she says, "they disappeared without a trace." Understanding her "to mean the 'trace' they disappeared without was me," Joe takes Trace as his last name (124). As a boy, Joe is taught to hunt by Hunters Hunter, and before leaving to Palestine he attempts to find Wild one last time in the woods. However, when he calls out, "You my mother?" asking that she "Give me a sign," he receives no response (178).

Without clear sense of his ancestral roots, Joe becomes vulnerable to constant reinvention and notes that by the time he meets Dorcas he had "changed into new seven times" (123). Like Violet, Joe seeks escape from the past, and thus they each find shelter in the fluid, dynamic nature of the City. Significantly, both do work focused upon beauty and reinvention. Violet becomes a hairdresser perhaps due to "all those years of listening to her rescuing grandmother" tell stories of Golden Gray's "carefully loved hair" (17). Joe starts out waiting tables where he learns to "sell trust" through careful attention; he masks whiskey to look like coffee and refreshes half-full glasses so customers do not have to ask for what they really want (122). This focus on outward appearances leads him to sell beauty products and, while on a casual house call, he meets Dorcas.

Like Violet and Joe, Dorcas is also an orphan. After her parents die in the St. Louis riots, she is taken in by Alice Manfred, her mother's sister. Alice is a strict disciplinarian who, despite resenting her own rigid upbringing, passes on suffocating ideas about female sexuality and "the damnation of pregnancy without marriageability" to Dorcas (76). She dresses her niece in conservative outfits, teaches her to avoid all white men, and warns her against the music that "was so lowdown you had to shut your windows and just suffer the summer sweat" (55–56). By isolating herself from the world, Alice becomes blind to Dorcas's insistent and reckless rebellion. With her best friend Felice, Dorcas alters her dowdy outfits and attends dance parties. But most importantly, she carries on an affair with Joe.

Caught in a static marriage with Violet, who has become increasingly distant and so obsessed with babies that she sleeps with a doll, Joe finds solace with Dorcas. Together they share stories of their orphaned childhoods, and Joe tells his young lover about his futile hunt for Wild. He showers Dorcas with gifts and takes her to nightclubs, but she soon becomes bored with his steady affection. She craves status among her peers, and because of their age difference, her affair with Joe must remain a secret. On the night of her death, she attends a party with Acton, her handsome new boyfriend. Unlike Joe, Acton tells Dorcas how to dress and fix her hair. Dorcas relishes these commands because to her they indicate that he cares about who she is and who she could be; as she notes, "I wanted to have a personality and with Acton I'm getting one" (190).

Joe tracks down Dorcas, and with the gun he once carried in the South, he shoots her as she dances with Acton. In the moments prior to finding her, Joe seems to confuse the object of his search. Though he follows Dorcas to a party, he assumes that he will find her by herself: "She'll be alone. Hardheaded. Wild" (182). His expectation that she will be alone and his reference to her as "Wild" indicate a conflation between Dorcas and his mother. Joe's love for Dorcas derives from his abandonment by Wild. By seeking his young lover, he completes his original hunt for his mother, and in killing Dorcas, he destroys a figure who represents his devastating childhood rejection.

Like Sethe, who must revisit the trauma of her past in order to move beyond it, both Joe and Violet must confront the history that led to this decisive moment. For Violet, this involves learning about Dorcas and discovering what qualities attracted Joe to her. She begins this search by visiting Alice, and the two begin an uneasy exchange. Initially, Alice is outraged by Violet's appearance at her doorstep, but she too is curious to unravel the mystery of Joe's love for Dorcas. The two women soon discover that they have much in common. Alice's husband left her for another woman, and like Violet, who has gained the nickname Violent following the episode at Dorcas's funeral, she seethed with rage and dreamt of mauling her husband's lover. In Violet, Alice finds a confidant and comrade, someone who shares her struggles as a black woman and who requires her most authentic self:

> The thing was how Alice felt and talked in her company. Not like she did with other people. With Violent she was impolite. Sudden. Frugal. No apology or courtesy seemed required or necessary between them. But something else was—clarity, perhaps. (83)

As in *Sula*, Morrison demonstrates how female friendship can be healing and restorative. Alice and Violet not only find comfort in their conversations but also experience the joys of laughter, which is "More complicated, more serious than tears" because it provides the foundation of survival based in joy (113).

In the first chapter of *Jazz*, the narrator promises a second murder, describing how Violet saw "another girl with four marcelled waves on each side of her head . . . and that's how that scandalizing threesome on Lenox Avenue began. What turned out different was who shot whom" (6). That girl with the marcelled waves is Felice, who comes to visit Joe and Violet to inquire about a ring she once loaned Dorcas. However, no scandal ensues; instead Felice finds Joe to be reflective and tender while Violet has regained a new clarity by destroying the part of herself that wanted to be "White. Light. Young again." She tells Felice that she killed that false self and "Then I killed the me that killed her" so what's left is just "Me" (208). The violent urge she once directed at Dorcas has at last found its necessary object, the inauthentic part of her own self.

Felice also supplies Violet and Joe with crucial information, explaining that Dorcas welcomed her own death by refusing to have an ambulance come or allowing herself to be taken to the hospital (209). Privately Felice tells Joe that Dorcas's dying wish was to convey a message to him: "There's only one apple . . . Just one. Tell Joe" (213). Dorcas here refers to a previous comment made by Joe in which he describes their love as the forbidden fruit from the Garden of Eden; "no point in picking the apple if you don't want to see how it tastes" (40). Dorcas's final words suggest that her love for Joe was both sincere and singular. While he may have been looking for a substitute for his mother, Dorcas regarded him as her true love. For this reason, she refuses to implicate him in her death.

The knowledge that Felice imparts to Joe liberates him, and he tells her that he and Violet are finally working on their relationship, noting that their progress is "Faster now, since you stopped by and told us what you did" (212). Rather than becoming another rival for Joe's affections, Felice befriends both him and Violet. She promises to bring some records over, and Violet insists on doing her hair for free. Like Sethe, who relives the moment of Beloved's death when Mr. Bodwin comes for Denver and directs her violence at him who she believes to be schoolteacher, the Traces relive their destructive encounter with

Dorcas through Felice. Empowered by a stronger sense of their authentic selves and the childhood motives that defined their dangerous need for love, Joe and Violet treat Felice as a gentle, inquisitive houseguest, a young woman who might learn from their own botched experiences with love and longing.

Because of this remarkable and healing shift in behavior, the narrator of *Jazz* must admit the mistake of anticipating scandal where instead there is only reconciliation:

> So I missed it altogether. I was sure one would kill the other . . . That the past was an abused record with no choice but to repeat itself at the crack . . . Busy, they were, busy being original, complicated, changeable—human, I guess, you'd say, while I was the predictable one, confused in my solitude into arrogance, thinking my space, my view was the only one. (220)

These concluding reflections suggest the unusual perspective of the narrator, a voice that is intimate and knowing, yet ultimately fails to predict the actions of the text's characters.

Many critics have offered various theories about the identity of the narrator, suggesting that it is an observant neighbor or an omniscient presence who is related to the novel's opening epigraph, "I am the name of the sound/and the sound of the name/I am the sign of the letter/and the designation of the division." This passage is derived from *The Nag Hammadi*, a collection of Gnostic scriptures from the second or third century. The epigraph relates to the title of the novel, *Jazz*, which may be understood as both the sound and the name of a musical form. This reference to artistic form supports John Leonard's conclusion that the narrator "is the book itself, this physical object, our metatext."[18] Morrison has confirmed this interpretation, stating that *Jazz* is "a love song of a book talking to the reader."[19]

In the concluding pages of the novel, the narrator describes the love of Violet and Joe, who "whisper to each other under the covers" and together share memories of their pasts (228). Where once outward appearances reigned supreme, now they do not even need to look at one another to know and trust their love. While Joe and Violet have come to an understanding of one another that forgives and endures, the narrator pines for a lover, confessing:

*That I have loved only you, surrendered my whole self reckless to you
and nobody else. That I want you to love me back and show it to me.
That I love the way you hold me, how close you let me be to you. I like
your fingers on and on, lifting, turning . . . If I were able I'd say it. Say
make me, remake me. You are free to do it and I am free to let you
because look, look. Look where your hands are. Now.* (229)

The physical references suggest that the narrator is the book lying
in the reader's hands and their love is consummated only through the
participatory engagement between text and reader. Morrison concludes with a startling ode to reading, suggesting that like love, this
process is dynamic, transformative, and even healing.

In 1993 Morrison received the Nobel Prize for Literature, becoming
the first African American writer to win the most prestigious literary
prize in the world. The Nobel committee praised her as a writer "who,
in novels characterized by visionary force and poetic import, gives life
to an essential aspect of American reality." Morrison had received
numerous other accolades, including Italy's highest literary award, the
Chianti Ruffino Antico Fattore, in 1990 (this was the first time the
honor was bestowed upon a black person or a woman). As a result, her
international reputation surged throughout Europe, Africa, and South
America. However, the Nobel Prize confirmed her position as one of
the most important American writers of all time.

That November Morrison traveled to Stockholm, Sweden, to accept
the prize, noting to the award committee that female winners should be
given more advance notice because they must find an appropriate dress
and shoes and cannot just rent a tuxedo.[20] Morrison was helped by
designer Bill Blass, who outfitted her in a regal dress. Although she
invited President Clinton and Salman Rushdie to accompany her, both
declined, and she instead made the trip with an entourage that included
her son Harold Ford, book critic John Leonard, Nobel Prize–winning
playwright Wole Soyinka, and African American Studies scholar Henry
Louis Gates Jr., among many others. She accepted the prize with a strong
sense of its meaning for other African American women writers. As she
reflected, "I felt a lot of 'we' excitement. It was as if the whole category of
'female writer' and 'black writer' had been redeemed. I felt I represented
a whole world of women who either were silenced or who had never

received the imprimatur of the established literary world."[21] Though she later noted that the prize would not help her write her next novel, it certainly would inspire other writers like her to believe that their stories could achieve equal recognition and praise.

In her opening banquet speech, Morrison hailed the writers who preceded her into the Nobel hall, writers whose "astonishing brilliance . . . challenged and nurtured my own." She also thanked her sister writers, one of whom called to tell her that "the prize that is yours is also ours and could not have been placed in better hands." Finally, Morrison described "a new and much more delightful haunting than the one I felt upon entering: that is the company of Laureates yet to come," noting that the work of present and future writers promises new vistas and insights. Looking to past, present, and future writers, Morrison relished "what is for me a moment of grace."[22]

Her acceptance speech focused upon the power of language and narrative to create identity and community. She began by emphasizing how storytelling provides knowledge of the world and then segued into a parable familiar to many cultures involving a group of young people who visit an old blind woman. They bring her a bird and to test her wisdom they ask if it is living or dead. The woman responds by telling them that she does not know if it is living or dead, only that "It is in your hands."[23]

In her Nobel lecture, Morrison undertakes a rich interpretation of the story in which she understands the woman to be a writer and the bird a symbol of language. This reading depends on a notion of language as a living entity that is subject to death. The death of language does not mean the end of its common use but instead signifies censorship, dominance, and the suppression of difference and new ideas. For Morrison, language is dead when it promotes ignorance and despotism rather than cultivating the full range of human possibility. She further explains that all are responsible for such death, not simply those who wield social and political power. Children express themselves through acts of violence rather than through words while adults dismiss the rich possibilities of verbal communication to both explore and create meaning. By emphasizing the personal aspects of language, Morrison highlights how we are all purveyors of language and must foster its generative qualities rather than accept totalitarian language that does not allow or encourage exchange. All fields of knowledge and human interaction—law, politics, science, education, and the arts—must resist discourses of exclusion and dominance.

In her analysis of the dynamic potential of language, Morrison cites the story of the Tower of Babel. Its collapse has traditionally been understood to be a misfortune. Morrison, however, interprets the fall into many languages as a blessing because it ensures difference rather than a singular conception of heaven. Had the creators of the tower had the patience to learn other languages and hence understand the perspectives of others, they might have discovered a paradise in their own world, one which is "Complicated, demanding, yes, but a view of heaven as life; not heaven as post-life" (202).

For Morrison, the difference secured by the variability of language promises possibility. She concedes that although "language can never live up to life . . . its felicity is in its reach towards the ineffable" (203). The mere attempt to express the depths and complications of life produces knowledge that is fundamental to understanding our place and responsibility to the world. Morrison concludes by imagining the response of the young people who are frustrated with the blind woman's enigmatic answer. They admit that in fact there is no bird in their hands and they come to her bearing only their question and an awareness of the crisis of language that surrounds them. They charge her with giving them no narrative of her history that might help them to understand their own lives. Their request for a story, however, is answered not by the blind woman, but by themselves. In their demand for a narrative that might guide and direct them, they imagine one of their own—the story of a wagonload of slaves who arrive at an inn where they are offered cider, bread, and a steady look by a girl and a boy. The blind woman delights at their narrative and exclaims, "Look. How lovely it is, this thing we have done—together" (207).

The live response to Morrison's speech was astonishing. The audience rose to applaud not once but twice, an unprecedented reaction to a Nobel lecture. Writing about the event for the *Nation*, John Leonard observed, "there's never been such majesty. I wasn't the only wet-eyed New York smarty-pants proud to be a citizen of whatever country Toni Morrison comes from."[24] Following Morrison's speech, Cornel West noted that she had "shattered black invisibility" though Morrison might have remarked that such invisibility had never existed among the community of readers that have most mattered to her.[25]

Notes

1. Jean Strouse, "Toni Morrison's Black Magic," *Newsweek* (March 30, 1981): 52.

2. Toni Morrison, *Tar Baby* (New York: Plume, 1981), 18 (hereafter cited in text).

3. Thomas LeClair, "'The Language Must Not Sweat': A Conversation with Toni Morrison," in *Conversations with Toni Morrison*, ed. Danille Taylor-Guthrie (Jackson, MS: University Press of Mississippi, 1994), 122.

4. Amiri Baraka, "Introduction," in *Confirmation: An Anthology of African American Women*, eds. Amiri Baraka (LeRoi Jones) and Amina Baraka (New York: William Morrow and Company, Inc., 1983), 15.

5. Ibid., 19.

6. Toni Morrison, "Recitatif," in *Before Columbus Foundation Fiction Anthology: Selections from the American Book Awards 1980-1990*, eds. Ishmael Reed, Kathryn Trueblood, and Shawn Wong (New York: W. W. Norton, 1992), 445-46 (hereafter cited in text).

7. Margaret Croyden, "Toni Morrison Tries Her Hand at Playwriting," in *Conversations with Toni Morrison*, ed. Danille Taylor-Guthrie (Jackson, MS: University Press of Mississippi, 1994), 219.

8. Ibid., 220.

9. Ibid., 222.

10. Qtd. in Hilton Als, "Ghosts in the House: Profiles," *The New Yorker* (October 27, 2003): 74.

11. Herbert Mitgang, "For Morrison, Prize Silences Gossip," *New York Times* (April 1, 1988): B5.

12. Ibid.

13. Gloria Naylor, "A Conversation: Gloria Naylor and Toni Morrison," in *Conversations with Toni Morrison*, ed. Danille Taylor-Guthrie (Jackson, MS: University Press of Mississippi, 1994), 207.

14. Toni Morrison, *Beloved* (New York: Plume, 1987), 18 (hereafter cited in text).

15. Ann Hostetler, "Interview with Toni Morrison: 'The Art of Teaching,'" in *Toni Morrison: Conversations*, ed. Carolyn C. Denard (Jackson, MS: University Press of Mississippi, 2008), 199.

16. Toni Morrison, *Jazz* (New York: Plume, 1992), 8 (hereafter cited in text).

17. Ralph Ellison, *Shadow and Act* (New York: Vintage International, 1953), 246.

18. John Leonard, "Her Soul's High Song: Review of *Jazz*," *Nation* (May 25, 1992): 718.

19. Angels Carabi, "Nobel Laureate Toni Morrison Speaks about Her Novel *Jazz*," in *Toni Morrison: Conversations*, ed. Carolyn C. Denard (Jackson, MS: University Press of Mississippi, 2008), 95.

20. Jim Haskins, *Toni Morrison: Telling a Tale Untold* (Brookfield, CT: Twenty-First Century Books, 2003), 113.

21. Claudia Dreifus, "Chloe Wofford Talks about Toni Morrison," in *Toni Morrison: Conversations*, ed. Carolyn C. Denard (Jackson, MS: University Press of Mississippi, 2008), 98.

22. Toni Morrison, "Banquet Speech," Nobelprize.org (December 10, 1993).

23. Toni Morrison, "The Nobel Lecture in Literature," in *What Moves at the Margin: Selected Nonfiction*, ed. Carolyn C. Denard (Jackson, MS: University Press of Mississippi, 2008), 199 (hereafter cited in text).

24. John Leonard, "Travels with Toni," *The Nation* (January 17, 1994): 62.

25. Qtd. in Ibid., 62.

Chapter 6

LATER NOVELS

The joy of winning the Nobel Prize was eclipsed the following Christmas by a fire that burned down Morrison's home in Rockland County. Morrison originally bought the house in the town of Grand View-on-the-Hudson as a space entirely for herself. With her children now grown and starting families of their own, Morrison had chosen the former boathouse, which sat on the banks of the Hudson River, as a place where she could dedicate herself completely to writing. With its unassuming facade and lack of address number and mailbox, the house appeared simple and inconsequential. However, it was actually a multileveled building that had its own pier on the river and was filled with plants, books, and Morrison's most cherished possessions.

The fire began in the fireplace but leaped into the living room, burning up the dry pine needles left from the holiday festivities. Morrison was not home when it started, and by the time one of her sons came downstairs, the fire was already through the roof. He called the fire department, but because of the harsh winter, the water was frozen in the pipes. Morrison lost countless manuscripts, first-edition books by Emily Dickinson and William Faulkner, and plants she had nurtured for over twenty years. But the most painful losses included pictures of her children, grade school report cards, letters, and other pieces of family memorabilia. The loss was devastating, and for some months Morrison spoke only to people who had also had their houses burn down, a small circle that included writer Maxine Hong Kingston.

Morrison decided to rebuild her house. Unfortunately she could not use the more than $800,000 she received for the Nobel Prize for this purpose since she had placed the winnings in a restricted retirement account. The sorrow caused by the fire was exacerbated by her mother's death a few months later on February 17, the day before Morrison's sixty-third birthday. Though Ramah had been ailing for some time, her death was inevitably shocking. In only three months, Morrison experienced one of the highlights of her career and endured one of the most difficult times of her life. Amid such dramatic changes, Morrison again found peace in writing. Within a year, she was newly absorbed in her seventh novel, *Paradise*, and also began a long-standing partnership with celebrity talk show host Oprah Winfrey.

In 1996, Oprah launched her widely popular book club and announced that *Song of Solomon* would be the club's second selection. Less than a week later, Morrison's third novel became the number one best seller on *Publishers Weekly*'s trade paperback list while sales of her other books also rose. Morrison's publisher responded by dropping the hardcover prices of many of her novels, making her works accessible to a broader audience. *Time* magazine has called Oprah's Book Club "the greatest force in publishing today" as it propels even little-known writers to the top of best seller lists.[1] More than any other author, Morrison has reaped the benefits of the "Oprah effect." Her work has been showcased four times on the show; in addition to *Song of Solomon*, *Paradise* was chosen in 1998, *The Bluest Eye* in 2000, and *Sula* in 2002. On each occasion Morrison has been invited on air to discuss her work with a select group of audience members.

Critics note that Winfrey's approach to novels is based less in rigorous literary analysis than in finding points of personal relation to characters as if reading best functions as a type of therapy. However, unlike Jonathan Franzen, the author of *The Corrections* (2001), who scorned the book club as being too lowbrow despite agreeing to have his novel appear on the show, Morrison has been pleased to widen the audience for her works. Winfrey also seems to have benefited from the partnership as indicated by an exchange she recalled for her studio audience: "I called up Toni Morrison and I said, 'Do people tell you they have to keep going over the words sometimes?' and she said, 'That, my dear, is called reading.'"[2]

Although Winfrey never chose *Beloved* as a selection for her book club, the novel had a profound effect on her. Immediately after reading it, Oprah decided that she wanted to bring the novel to the screen so that she could share Sethe's story and the horrors of slavery with a wider audience. She pictured herself in the lead role and at this early stage even imagined Danny Glover as Paul D. Winfrey developed a script, penned in part by Morrison, and submitted it to a variety of directors. Academy Award winner Jonathan Demme agreed to direct the film, which was produced by Winfrey's film company, Harpo Productions. Morrison had little role in the filming of the movie. Though she did visit the set, she found that her comments were not especially useful. Initially reluctant to be involved in the project at all because she did not want to revisit the characters in *Beloved*, Morrison allowed Winfrey and Demme to produce the film as they saw fit.

After ten years of development, the movie version of *Beloved* was finally released in 1998. The film received significant publicity prior to its opening, including cover stories in both *Time* and *Vogue* as well as discussion on Winfrey's talk show. Critics were generally impressed with the movie, noting how Demme built upon the images of the novel through his careful attention to natural settings and animal life. Winfrey also received positive reviews for her performance, although some found Thandie Newton's interpretation of Beloved to be alienating. Despite all of the press surrounding the film, *Beloved* generated minimal revenue at the box office. This lack of interest in the movie may be understood as a response to its difficult subject matter, but as Margo Jefferson wrote in the *New York Times*, *Beloved*'s failure may also have reflected an uncomfortable contrast between Oprah and the subject matter of the film: "It's very tricky to filter a movie about the horrors of history through a triumphantly successful celebrity power broker. And it gets even trickier if that celebrity is black and the film is about slavery."[3]

Morrison did not focus on the disappointing reception of *Beloved* but instead moved on to other concerns. While *Jazz* was in production, Morrison's longtime editor, Robert Gottlieb, left Knopf to become the editor of the *New Yorker*. The loss was deeply felt by Morrison. Since *Sula*, Gottlieb had worked with her on all of her novels, carefully reviewing each one line by line. As she notes, his objective approach to her work made him an ideal reader and editor:

What made him good for me was a number of things: knowing what not to touch; asking all the questions you probably would have asked yourself had there been the time. Good editors are really the third eye. Cool. Dispassionate. They don't love you or your work; for me that is what is valuable—not compliments.[4]

Sonny Mehta became the president of Knopf, and because he was not as engaged with authors on a detailed textual level, he gave Morrison the option to choose her own line editor. She selected Erroll McDonald, an editor at Pantheon, a division of Random House. The two established an unusual method of working together that Morrison described in an interview: "What he does is write me long, interesting letters. And the letters contain information about what's strong, what's successful, what troubles him, what stands out as being really awful, that kind of thing. Which is what you want."[5] McDonald was instrumental in the publication of Random House editions of Morrison's Nobel lecture and "The Dancing Mind," the speech she delivered upon receiving the National Book Foundation Medal for Distinguished Contribution to American Letters in 1996.

Morrison sent the first one hundred pages of her new novel to McDonald, but the two had disagreements even about the title of the book. Although her seventh novel would be titled *Paradise*, Morrison wanted to call it *War*. However, many at Knopf were concerned that this title would alienate readers. Despite her misgivings, Morrison agreed to the change. Although *Paradise* was to be released in the spring of 1998, Morrison was pushed to complete the book early in order to capitalize on post-holiday book sales. In January she went on a publicity tour, an experience she did not enjoy given the constant travel and disruption of her routine. Fortunately, she was able to control some aspects of the tour. She avoided morning TV shows and insisted upon extended interviews in which she could substantially explore the issues raised in her novel. This was particularly important when discussing *Paradise* because the book incorporates substantial historical research.

In her study of the black towns that developed throughout the end of the nineteenth and the beginning of the twentieth century, Morrison came across an ad printed in a black newspaper that read "Come prepared or not at all."[6] This pithy call urged newly freed slaves and their descendants to create their own promised land within the western territories. Exploring issues of exclusion and acceptance, *Paradise* describes the invasion of a local convent by a group of men who believe that the refuge for wandering women has become a threat to their town. This encounter is derived from a convent of black nuns Morrison learned about while she was on a research trip in Brazil. The nuns, who cared for abandoned children, practiced Catholicism on the first floor and a form of voodoo in the basement. According to the story, which has been disproved, a group of local men attacked the convent and killed the nuns. Despite being no more than a fabrication, the story became the basis for Morrison's study of how communities construct narratives for political and social purposes.

Paradise spans nearly one hundred years of history and mythology and demonstrates the ways in which stories change to fit present needs. In this sweeping novel of a town's rise and fall, Morrison returns to themes of community and the destabilizing but necessary role of social pariahs. Chronologically, *Paradise* begins in the 1880s when a collection of ex-slaves from Louisiana and Mississippi ventures west to settle the Oklahoma territory. Led by nine patriarchs, the group nearly starves before arriving at the all-black town of Fairly in Oklahoma. However, in an event later named the Disallowing, the travelers are provided with food but are told they must move on. They are not welcome in Fairly because of their dark skin, what the informal town historian Patricia Best calls "8-rock," referring to a deep level in coal mines. Pat characterizes the settlers as "Blue black people, tall and graceful, whose clear, wide eyes gave no sign of what they really felt about those who weren't 8-rock like them."[7]

The pioneering families continue their journey west, at last establishing their own all-black town of Haven in 1890. To mark their new home, the town founders build a communal Oven where all are welcome to bake bread. Haven is built upon a deep ethos of cooperation and unity, but these values prove to be problematic as the town reenacts a dangerous form of exclusivity. In particular, light-skinned townspeople like Pat are shunned for manifesting the impurity associated with racial mixing and women are consigned to strict domestic roles that bar them from participating in the governance of the town. As

Reverend Misner, a relative newcomer, notes, the town so emphasizes the preservation of certain traditions, including racial continuity, that "rather than children, they wanted duplicates" (161).

Although Haven thrives for a few decades, during the 1930s many young people begin leaving in large part due to World War II. When the prominent Morgan twins, Deacon and Steward, return from the war, they are outraged by Haven's state of neglect. They decide to pack up the remnants of the town, including the Oven, and search for a place to begin again. Along with fourteen other families, they settle in an isolated area ninety miles from the nearest town and seventeen miles from a massive old house known locally as the Convent. The townspeople name their new home Ruby, after the Morgan sister who died during the journey.

Despite the establishment of a whole new community, there are clear signs that Ruby is weakening. The recent birth of four lame children to Jeff and Sweetie Fleetwood suggests that the town's insularity may be responsible for the children's defects. The wealthy and influential bank owners and town patriarchs, Deacon and Steward, are both childless; the former lost his two sons in Vietnam and the latter was never able to have children with his wife, Dovey. Aware that there are problems in Ruby, but unwilling to confront how the town's isolation and rigid hierarchy weaken it as a whole, the male leaders of Ruby direct their rage and frustration toward the inhabitants of the Convent.

The Convent, formerly owned by an embezzler, is decorated with pornographic ornaments—doorknobs in the shape of nipples, ashtrays built like vaginas, and statues of naked women. The embezzler went to jail before he could enjoy his raunchy home, and the mansion was taken over by nuns who used it as a school for Native American girls. Later the Convent becomes a haven for troubled and lost women from Ruby as well as from more distant locations. When Mavis, the first of these women, arrives, the Convent houses only two people, the ancient and bedridden Mother Superior, also known as Mary Magna, and Connie, her caretaker, who always wears sunglasses and lives off the money she makes selling hot peppers, spicy relishes, and other potent concoctions. Born in Brazil, Connie was stolen as an infant from the slums of Rio by the nuns and raised at the Convent. Her deep attachment to Mary Magna demonstrates the power of emotional bonds and active caretaking over biological connections between mother and child. In sharp contrast to the founding ideology of Ruby, the relationships at the Convent indicate that love and loyalty do not require blood ties of family and racial identification.

Morrison begins *Paradise* with the sentence "They shoot the white girl first." By the time the men from Ruby arrive to execute their destructive rampage, there are five women living in the Convent. Significantly, however, the second paragraph of the novel describes the attackers thus: "They are nine, over twice the number of the women they are obliged to stampede or kill" (3). This sentence implies that there are four, not five, women in the Convent, which Morrison carefully introduces in separate chapters, titled with their names. This glaring discrepancy reveals that as in *Jazz*, this narrator is also unreliable. Later descriptions of the origin myths of Haven and Ruby boldly contradict one another; at one point the settlers initially heading west to Oklahoma number "one hundred and fifty-eight freedmen," but in another account they are described as "all seventy-nine," exactly half the number first given (13, 95). No logical answer explains this difference, which points to Morrison's overarching concern with the mutability of historical narratives. The stories of a nation or a community become mythologized through deliberate omissions and exaggerations that then constitute a master narrative that enshrines a certain identity for its citizens. The mythic history of Ruby involves a story of racial oppression and fierce will that allowed a people to create a home in opposition to discriminatory forces. Any narrative that threatens this story and the integrity of Ruby must therefore be eradicated. By placing a blatant historical contradiction on the first page of *Paradise*, Morrison cautions readers to interpret the stories of Ruby and its townspeople as constructions based on specific desires and needs, not as reflections of historical fact.

To return to the opening line of *Paradise*, it is important to note that while Morrison provides a substantial history for each woman living in the Convent, she avoids any mention of their racial identity. This approach reflects her exploration of what she describes in the 1997 essay "Home" as her desire to conceptualize home as "a-world-in-which-race-does-*not*-matter."[8] Significantly, her aim is not to banish race and thereby form a color-blind utopia where difference disappears, but rather she seeks a way to "convert a racist house into a race-specific yet nonracist home," asking, "How to enunciate race while depriving it of its lethal cling?" and thereby how to fashion "race-specific, race-free language."[9]

The concept of home is the central point of exploration in *Paradise*: What constitutes a home? Who is welcome there? What role does race occupy in a home space? Is paradise a world in which everyone is of the same race? Without racial difference, does discrimination based on social status disappear? Or can paradise include racial difference? Though Ruby is founded on a history of racial discrimination, specifically through the Disallowing, the town reenacts racial hierarchy by prizing 8-rock blood. By contrast, the women of the Convent succeed in creating an environment in which race is incidental. They are each defined by strong character traits and by key experiences—Mavis is haunted by the bewildering death of her infant twins, Gigi's seductive facade belies a romantic streak, Seneca's neediness reflects her childhood abandonment, and Pallas is nearly mute with grief after her boyfriend takes up with her mother. Racial identification is made only when the men arrive at the Convent, suggesting that the physical violence they inflict is intimately tied to their need for racial classification. In sharp opposition to the Convent, the men of Ruby depend on race as a way of defining and enforcing the borders of their town. Similarly, because they fear racial pollution, Pat notes, "everything that worries them must come from women" (217). This terror accounts for the objectifying femininity prized in Ruby, a form of womanhood that prizes submissiveness and silence.

The rage produced by the Disallowing and the fierce desire to preserve Ruby as a haven for African Americans leads to a dangerous form of isolation. Outsiders and anyone who advocates change are treated with suspicion if not overt hostility. The townspeople of Ruby are not only wary of the women living in the Convent, but there are heated debates between younger and older generations that point to critical issues about how or even if community values should evolve. One of the central points of contention is the motto emblazoned at the base of the Oven. Elder members of the community insist that the motto is "Beware the Furrow of his Brow" and warns of the might of a wrathful

God (86). The younger generation, influenced by the rhetoric of the civil rights and Black Power movements, argue that the motto is better read as "Be the Furrow of His Brow" (87). They criticize a motto that enshrines a dangerous god who requires the townspeople "To always be ducking and diving, trying to look out every minute in case He's getting ready to throw something at us, keep us down" (84).

To the horror of the town elders, the younger inhabitants of Ruby assert that the authority once accorded to a divine being is theirs to claim. Steward ends the discussion by threatening violence to anyone who attempts to change the motto on the Oven. He sees only disrespect in the claims of the young people and is dismissive of Reverend Misner's belief that because "they do know the Oven's value . . . they want to give it new life" (86). For both the Morgan twins, the values of the town are necessarily unchangeable and absolute. They allow for no deviation from the traditions of the past and will resort to violence in order to uphold their inflexible rule of law. Later, Anna Flood, a woman with more progressive ideas and who has lived away from Ruby, privately reflects that the motto would be better expressed as "Be the Furrow of Her Brow" (159). While this suggestion remains unvoiced, it expresses a central concern of the text, the way in which patriarchal institutions ignore female forms of divinity.

The conflict over Ruby's motto, which in part concerns the nature of God's power and its relation to humanity, is also examined in a specifically religious context. The two leading reverends of the community, Reverend Misner and Reverend Pulliam, describe in separate sermons very different approaches to God and divine love. Pulliam, an older man who aligns with the conservative values of the Morgans, contends that God's love must be earned and that "God is not interested in you. He is interested in love and the bliss it brings to those who understand and share that interest" (142). According to Pulliam, God's love is conferred only by rigidly adhering to the patriarchal teachings of the church.

The younger Reverend Misner, who moved to Ruby after participating in the protests inspired by Dr. Martin Luther King, responds to Pulliam by taking the cross from the back wall of the church and carrying it to the front altar. Without saying a word, Misner hopes to impart through this bold gesture his belief that the crucifixion empowers individuals by moving humans from backstage to the spotlight, from muttering in the wings to the principal role in the story of their lives. This execution made it possible to respect—freely, not in fear—one's self and one another. Which was what love was: unmotivated respect. All of which testified not to a peevish Lord who was His own love but to one who enabled human love. Not for His own glory—never. God loved the way humans loved one another; loved the way humans loved themselves; loved the genius on the cross who managed to do both and die knowing it. (146)

Misner's conception of God is premised upon the radical notion "that not only is God interested in you; He is you" (147). This approach to the divine reflects Morrison's study of the Gnostic Gospels, a collection of writings about the teachings of Jesus, written around the second century AD. While at Princeton, Morrison developed a deep friendship with Elaine Pagels, a noted scholar of early Christianity and author of numerous books on the Gnostic Gospels. Pagels's work explains that these writings were not included in the standard biblical canon because they presented ideas considered dangerous to the authority of the early church fathers. Among other teachings, the Gnostic Gospels explain that salvation is located in the individual, not in an external divinity, and highlight the importance of female figures in religious practice.

Though printed without citation, the epigraph of *Paradise* is taken from "Thunder, Perfect Mind," a poem discovered among the Gnostic manuscripts at Nag Hammadi in 1945. Religious scholars describe the voice of this text as a female revealer who embodies opposing qualities and possesses transformative powers. Morrison cites the conclusion of the poem in which the speaker admits the pleasures of sinful behavior while also seeking the salvation of her listeners:

For many are the pleasant forms which exist in
numerous sins,
and incontinencies,
and disgraceful passions
and fleeting pleasures,
which (men) embrace until they become
sober
and go up to their resting place.

And they will find me there,
and they will live,
and they will not die again.

This passage is best read in conjunction with the character of Connie or Consolata. Her supernatural powers suggest that she represents the female divinity described by the Gnostic texts. Connie is able to resurrect the dead by "stepping in" dying bodies, but she is also vulnerable to fundamentally human desires (247). She has a passionate affair with Deek Morgan that abruptly ends when Deek becomes unsettled by the depth of her desire; at one point she bites him, drawing blood.

By the time Mavis and the other women arrive at the Convent, Connie has retreated into a deep isolation that is broken only by her unflagging dedication to Mary Magna. However, she occupies a unique position among the women of the Convent that highlights her almost Christ-like appeal: "This sweet, unthreatening old lady who seemed to love each one of them best; who never criticized, who shared everything but needed little or no care; required no emotional investment; who listened; who locked no doors and accepted each as she was" (262). This description echoes Misner's claim that God loves humanity with a type of unconditional love that recognizes individual difference.

At the end of the novel, Connie assumes a powerful leadership role toward the women. She orders them to lie naked on the floor, and after tracing the outlines of their bodies, she says:

My child body, hurt and soil, leaps into the arms of a woman who teach me my body is nothing my spirit everything. I agreed her until I met another. My flesh so hungry for itself it ate him. When he fell away the woman rescue me from my body again. Twice she saves it. When her body sicken I care for it in every way flesh works . . . After she is dead I can not get past that. My bones on hers the only good thing . . . No different from the man. My bones on his the only true thing. So I wondering where is the spirit lost in this? It is true, like bones. It is good, like bones. One sweet, one bitter. Where is it lost? Hear me, listen. Never break them in two. Never put one over the other. Eve is Mary's mother. Mary is the daughter of Eve. (263)

There are a number of key ideas expressed in this passage. Though Connie has divine powers, she draws her strength from relationships with humans, specifically the bond she had with her mother, Mary Magna, and the affair she had with Deek. Both provide experiences of love that profoundly shape her and which, importantly, include aspects of pain. There is no love, no joy without bitterness; this union of opposites underscores as well how Connie merges human and divine qualities. Connie also cautions her listeners not to "put one over the other," that is, not to prioritize one form of love over the other. Maternal love and sexual love must not be conceived as rivals, but instead as elements of a continuous and evolving experience. One encounter with love leads to another, and in this way Connie is both healed and heals others. By invoking a direct line of descent between Eve and Mary, Connie confirms that transgression can lead to grace, that sin can lead to salvation. The women of the Convent have all encountered heartache and struggle, and Connie here promises them renewal. However, as they lie in the outlines on the floor, they must turn inward for such redemption because, as affirmed by the Gnostic Gospels, divinity lies within each of them.

Although the opening pages of *Paradise* describe the violent attack on the Convent by the men of Ruby, the end of the novel presents each of the women making peace with the figures of their past; Mavis has breakfast with her once vicious daughter, Pallas revisits her mother's house but ignores the woman who betrayed her so that she can collect a pair of shoes, Gigi skinny-dips with a lover, and Seneca is discovered by her mother though she no longer needs the latter's love. When Misner and Anna return to the Convent to see for themselves the sight of the rampage, there are no dead bodies and no signs of violence, only an abandoned house. This absence leaves open the possibility that no murder occurred at all, and it is only the story of the annihilation of the Convent women that the patriarchs of Ruby needed for their deeply flawed paradise to survive.

Of all of Morrison's novels, *Paradise* received the most scathing reviews. Michiko Kakutani in the *New York Times* called the novel a "contrived, formulaic book that mechanically pits men against women, old against young, the past against the present" while David Gates in *Newsweek* wrote "we're asked to swallow too many contrivances . . . But the main problem is that there are too many characters to keep straight and too few to care about."[10] Reviewers entirely ignored the discrepancies provided about the history of Haven and Ruby and made opposing assertions as to the identity of the white girl. However, as Ron David notes, these reviews only highlight Morrison's approach to the artificiality of constructed narratives and the ways in which mythologies depend on the acceptance of glaring omissions. David argues that the mistakes of the novel are deliberate because "*Paradise* is a myth-in-progress . . . The plot isn't realistic because TM wanted it to be over the edge—like a myth! The novel 'tries out' every kind of myth, from Biblical and Greek to witch hunts and cartoons and combinations of all of the above."[11] The experimental and even frustrating nature of *Paradise* demonstrates Morrison's commitment to narrative innovation. While she returns to certain themes and ideas in her work, she does not rewrite familiar plots or characters. Each of her novels presents a unique and compelling set of issues, both thematically and stylistically, that consistently challenge her audience to reach beyond familiar reading patterns.

Morrison's next novel, *Love* (2003), also destabilizes conventional perspectives through its exploration of the complex relationships of the Cosey family and the decline of their beachfront resort, a once luxurious vacation destination for African Americans during the mid- to late twentieth century. *Love* again highlights the elegance of Morrison's prose and her firm dedication to writing for and about the black community. A much shorter and less dense novel than *Paradise*, *Love* echoes many of the ideas and concerns explored in *Sula*. The central plot focuses upon the childhood friendship between two girls from opposite social backgrounds. Christine is the light-skinned granddaughter of the wealthy and powerful Bill Cosey, whose hotel and resort caters to an elite black clientele. Her best friend, Heed the Night Johnson, comes from a large family of poor cannery workers. Despite their differences, the two "shared stomachache laughter, a secret language, and knew as they slept together that one's dreaming was the same as the other one's."[12] Their friendship is violently disrupted when the widowed Cosey decides to marry the eleven-year-old Heed. As the richest and most influential man in the Up Beach community, Cosey is free to fulfill his perverse desire even as it breeds deep discord among the women of his household.

Much like *Jazz* and *Paradise*, *Love* explores another version of paradise through the creation of Cosey's Hotel and Resort. As a vacation
destination, Cosey's Hotel allows visitors to become their best selves,
mirroring the seductive qualities of *Jazz*'s New York with a tacit understanding that such fantasies will not last beyond a weekend's dalliance
or at most a summer of quiet indiscretion. Even after the resort is abandoned, L, the novel's narrator, comments, *"if you look inside, the hotel
seems to promise you ecstasy and the company of all your best friends"* (7).
As in *Paradise*, Cosey's Hotel provides its guests with the comfort and
pride of Ruby's all-black environment, but without the complications
of its governance and management. However, behind the seeming paradise of Cosey's Hotel and its promise of "The best good time" lies danger because its patron relies upon an oppressive and divisive approach
to women (34).

With its stylish clientele, scrupulous attention to detail, and sump-
tuous menu overseen by L, Cosey's Hotel presents a fantastic image of
black self-determination and prosperity. However, its luxuries are with-
held from the townspeople, who are prevented from using the hotel's
facilities. Local families hoping to celebrate a wedding at the hotel are
refused accommodation despite having the money to pay. Even after
such rejections, the townspeople concede that it is for the best since
they do not have the clothes and style of the other guests. The hotel
figures most prominently as a symbol of black potential, becoming a
promise of the future if not a lived reality: "it was enough to watch the
visitors, admire their cars and the quality of their luggage; to listen to
the distant music and dance to it in the dark . . . It was enough to know
Bill Cosey's Hotel and Resort was there" (41). The townspeople accept
their exile from paradise as normative, savoring the luxury of Cosey's
Resort and Hotel as a fantasy of possibility rather than as a tangible
part of their lives. While Eden is not theirs to enjoy, its existence is
guaranteed by Cosey's Hotel in much the same way that the supreme
power of its owner offers the specter of self-determination and wealth
for a poor and largely disenfranchised population.

In contrast to this image of a near but unattainable Eden is the paradise created and occupied by Christine and Heed. Perfection is their
reality, not a world they must observe and covet from afar. In one
another's company, the two girls do not have desires that they cannot

fulfill between themselves. For them, there is no understanding or even recognition of deprivation as a condition of life. The two complete one another entirely. Speaking of Heed, L notes that "she belonged to Christine and Christine belonged to her" (105). The two exist in a unified harmony that rejects May's disapproval of Heed's low-class background and ignores the sharp difference in skin color between them. In the childhood world of Christine and Heed, color and class are not meaningful categories of social identity; in fact, the only identity that exists is their united selfhood.

This paradise is destroyed by Bill Cosey. Although his marriage to Heed marks the full disintegration of their friendship, he instigates their breakup during an afternoon in 1940. The two girls have planned to take a picnic lunch to the beach, but on their way Heed goes back to retrieve the jacks left in Christine's room. While dancing to the music coming from the hotel, Heed encounters Cosey, who asks for her name and touches her nipple, or as the narrator qualifies, "the place under her swimsuit where a nipple will be if the circled dot on her chest ever changes." Bewildered by the encounter and the "burning, tingling" on her chest, Heed forgets the jacks and runs to tell Christine what Cosey has done (191). Rather than describe this critical exchange, Heed finds her friend with perplexing vomit stains on her swimming suit. Heed falsely concludes that "Christine knows what happened and it made her vomit" and comes to believe that there is something deeply wrong with her. However, Christine vomits not because of Heed but because rather than wait, she chased after Heed and saw her grandfather, fresh from his encounter with Heed, masturbating in her room. She vomits, "ashamed of her grandfather and of herself." Although she has done no wrong, Christine is aware that her presence has precipitated Cosey's act. She remembers his ominous presence from the night before: "When she went to bed that night, his shadow had booked the room. She didn't have to glance at the window . . . to know that an old man's solitary pleasure lurked there" (192).

Cosey's sexualization of the two girls profoundly changes their relationship. As objects of sexual desire, they are both overcome by shame and guilt for having elicited such a response from Cosey. This leads to a lasting silence between them as neither feels comfortable sharing their experiences of that summer day with the other. Once Cosey selects Heed as his wife, friendship turns into rivalry as the two compete for Cosey's affection and struggle to understand their new positions in his household. Cosey literally buys Heed from her parents, treating her as a commodity, not a person. His decision to marry Heed suggests his incestuous desire for Christine but also points to a disturbing quest for power. He explains that "he wanted to raise her and couldn't wait to watch her grow. That the steady, up-close observation most men don't know the pleasure of kept him not just true but lively" (148). While raising and watching a child grow is precisely what a father does for a daughter, an experience Cosey could have enjoyed with his granddaughter living at home, Cosey seeks to combine the duties of a father with the privileges of a lover. He fuses the two primary roles men have in relation to women, that of father and sexual partner, and thereby consolidates an unprecedented degree of power.

In doing so, Cosey creates an environment of rivalry and hostility among the women in his house while also degrading them all. Christine is banished to Maple Valley, a boarding school, after it becomes clear that the former friends cannot peacefully coexist in the same household. Cosey continues to treat his wife as a child, spanking her at the dining room table when she misbehaves in front of his dinner guests. May, Christine's mother, directs all her hatred at Heed, whom she perceives as hopelessly low-class. Without her daughter and widowed by the death of Cosey's son Billy, she works tirelessly in the hotel, but Cosey barely acknowledges her presence. She accepts her daughter's departure to boarding school because pleasing Cosey is more important than mothering her child. As L notes of May, "*Her whole life was making sure those Cosey men had what they wanted. The father more than the son, the father more than her own daughter*" (102). Significantly, none of the women direct their rage at Cosey. Following the spanking, Heed burns Christine's bed. Like May blaming Heed for Cosey's misbehavior, Heed attacks Christine rather than recognize Cosey's guilt. By sabotaging female relationships, these women destroy the powerful potential of their unity and reinforce Cosey's control over them.

Even after Cosey dies, the women are unable to set aside their hatred. In fact their feud is embittered by the ambiguous will Cosey scrawled on a hotel menu. He leaves the majority of his estate to his "sweet Cosey child" (88). Both Christine and Heed lay claim to this title; as his granddaughter, Christine is a Cosey child, but Heed always called her husband Papa, suggesting that she too may be the true recipient of his will. Although the law comes down in Heed's favor, Christine makes plans to appeal the ruling. At the start of the novel, the two are living together in the same house though on separate floors. Following a series of ruinous affairs, Christine returns to her childhood home, but without the means to live independently she moves in with her ailing mother and Heed. Once May dies, Christine takes on the duties of the household, cooking elaborate meals that she knows Heed will hate. In a striking reversal from their upbringing, the well-educated Cosey daughter serves the woman born into poverty.

This uneasy truce is broken by the arrival of Junior Viviane, a young woman who responds to an advertisement Heed has issued for a personal assistant. Having escaped an impoverished home as well as an abusive juvenile correctional facility, Junior represents a bold new type of "nineties women" that L disparages in the opening pages of the novel, women who "straddle chairs and dance crotch out on television" (3–4). Though Heed is appalled by Junior's outrageous clothes and her haughty tone, she hires her with the stated intention of compiling a history of the Cosey family. Junior takes an immediate liking to the portrait of Bill Cosey that adorns Heed's bedroom. In him, she sees "A handsome man with a G.I. Joe chin and a reassuring smile that pledged endless days of hot, tasty food; kind eyes that promised to hold a girl steady on his shoulder while she robbed apples from the highest branch" (30). Junior's view of Cosey demonstrates how his image reflects the needs and desires of those around him. He becomes a figure of malleable complexity, both a pillar of the Up Beach community and a manipulative, greedy pervert. For Junior, Cosey is a coconspirator, someone who will help her steal from Heed and Christine. Throughout the novel, she looks to his image as a source of comfort, fabricating his presence in the same way that the Up Beach community made him into a fantasy of black empowerment.

While employed by Heed, Junior begins an affair with Romen, a teenage boy who does yard work for the Cosey women. Romen is the grandson of Vida and Sandler Gibbons. Because Vida's job at the hotel saved her from a life of drudgery at the local cannery, she reveres Cosey. Sandler briefly worked as a waiter at the resort but spent most of his life in a supervisory position at the cannery. This distance afforded him the opportunity to pursue a tentative friendship with Cosey, who one day asked Sandler to join him on a fishing trip. Despite the over fifty-year age difference between them, Sandler agreed to accompany him and thereby learned intimate details about the town patriarch. Cosey tells Sandler about his deep love for his deceased son, Billy, with whom he had a relationship that was "More like pals than father and son" (43). He also confesses that his father, known by the nickname Dark, once made him watch a house until a certain man came out; the man was later dragged through the streets behind a horse wagon. Dark amassed a fortune by working as a courthouse informer and bequeathed his wealth to Cosey, who then invested in the hotel. Cosey's success is not derived from hard work alone but is built upon the betrayal and deception of his father.

In a novel overshadowed by the greed and perversity of Cosey, Sandler and Romen provide a marked respite from his patriarchal authority and damaging effect on women. Romen is first introduced in the back room of a house party. He has joined a posse of boys in the gang rape of Pretty Faye, a teenage girl. When it is his turn with the girl, the last of seven, Romen "watched in wonder as his hands moved to the headboard. The knot binding her right wrist came undone as soon as he touched it and her hand fell over the bedside" (46–47). Romen wraps the girl in a blanket and escorts her out of the house, where she is taken by two friends. His friends upbraid him for what they perceive to be his cowardice, finally beating him in the street though they save his face so that the marks of their abuse do not show. When he meets Junior at the Cosey home, Romen is entirely friendless. However, their sexual relationship radically transforms his social status as his schoolmates detect a new confidence in him and a scorn for his former friends: "When he approached the lockers that first day, they knew. And those who didn't he told—in a way. Anybody who needed to get drunk, or tie somebody up, or required the company of a herd, was a punk" (114).

Similarly aware of a sudden change to his grandson, Sandler decides to speak with Romen about the dangers and responsibilities of sex as well as the importance of finding the right woman. He warns him away from a relationship based entirely on physical pleasure and with a woman who "makes you feel uneasy," as Junior with her voracious sexual appetite does. Sandler further explains, "A good man is a good thing, but there is nothing in the world better than a good good woman. She can be your mother, your wife, your girlfriend, your sister, or somebody you work next to. Don't matter. You find one, stay there. You see a scary one, make tracks" (154–55). Sandler's advice anticipates the end of Romen's relationship with Junior, who abandons the Cosey women at the deserted hotel. Significantly, it is Romen who returns to rescue them, saving them just as he saved Pretty Faye.

Sandler's remarks about the importance of finding connection with a woman can be applied to the female as well as the male characters of the novel. The demise of Christine and Heed's friendship results from their failure to value one another. In their final, conciliatory conversation, Christine acknowledges that both she and Heed allowed themselves to be enslaved to men. She states, "Well, it's like we started out being sold, got free of it, then sold ourselves to the highest bidder" (185). Christine's comment can refer both to the historical condition of black women within antebellum slavery as well as to the specific circumstances of their lives. After leaving her childhood home, Christine finds herself in a series of exploitative relationships with men. While living in an upscale whorehouse, she observes:

> As in Maple Valley, everyone had a role and a matron ruled the stage. She hadn't escaped from anything. Maple Valley, Cosey's Hotel, Manila's whorehouse—all three floated in sexual tension and resentment; all three insisted on confinement; in all three status was money. And all were organized around the pressing needs of men. (92)

Just as Heed becomes consumed by her relationship with Cosey, so Christine and the various women she encounters are driven by a compulsion to establish lasting heterosexual partnerships at the expense of their relationships with women. Like May, who poisons her relationship with her daughter in order to maintain a glorified image of Cosey, Christine is willing to sacrifice family and self-respect to preserve the illusion of domestic harmony. She tolerates the adultery of her various male partners and while involved in the Black Power Movement, she agrees to have an abortion since "Revolutions needed men—not fathers" (164). While men are unencumbered by the most basic of family responsibilities, women are expected to attend to male needs and desires, and as Christine notes, they largely do so of their own free will.

At the conclusion of the novel, Heed and Christine make peace though their reconciliation requires a violent confrontation. Christine chases Heed and Junior to the abandoned hotel where Heed hopes to find old menus that she can use to forge a new will naming her as the sole beneficiary of Cosey's estate. Surprised by Christine's arrival, Heed accidentally falls halfway through broken floorboards. Junior then bolts from the attic, taking the only car left at the hotel and leaving the two Cosey women to fend for themselves. Rather than continue their feud, Christine tends to Heed's injuries and they discuss their once blissful childhood and its eventual bitterness. Christine concludes, "We could have been living our lives hand in hand instead of looking for Big Daddy everywhere" (189). The dialogue between them lacks quotations, suggesting both a return to their original fused state and the possibility that their conversation is no more than a fantasy. When Romen arrives, he finds one alive and one dead, but Morrison does not specify which has passed. The dialogue between the women continues even as one lies dead in the Cosey house. Though death has claimed one of the Cosey women, the strength drawn from their powerful friendship abides.

While *Love* received somewhat mixed reviews as critics struggled to understand if Cosey's marriage to Heed is best understood as satire or as a commentary on the dangers of totalizing male power, her most recent novel, *A Mercy*, has been hailed as a return to form. After disparaging both *Paradise* and, to a lesser extent, *Love*, Kakutani in the *New York Times* wrote, "Ms. Morrison has rediscovered an urgent, poetic voice that enables her to move back and forth with immediacy and ease between the worlds of history and myth, between ordinary daily life and the realm of fable."[13] The shortest of all her novels, *A Mercy* required years of research to provide credence to its seventeenth-century setting.

Influenced in particular by the history book *White Cargo* (2008), Morrison became fascinated with the nonracial origin of slavery in the early colonies. Through her study of early American settlers in *A Mercy*, Morrison seeks "to remove race from slavery." She notes that "the only difference between African slaves and European or British slaves was that the latter could run away and melt into the population, but if you were black you were noticeable."[14] White slaves were most often considered indentured servants who theoretically could work off their passage to the New World though they were often enslaved for life.

In her study of American colonial history, Morrison learned that race became a meaningful category of social identity primarily after Bacon's Rebellion, an uprising that occurred in Virginia in 1676. Led by wealthy planter Nathaniel Bacon, it marked one of the first instances in which poor blacks and whites were united in common cause. The possibility of such cross-racial coalition frightened the ruling class and led to new laws that protected white privilege and linked African ancestry to slave status. One of the main characters in *A Mercy*, Jacob Vaark, an enterprising Anglo-Dutch trader, reflects upon the stringent laws enacted to discourage alliances across racial and class divides:

> By eliminating manumission, gatherings, travel and bearing arms for black people only; by granting license to any white to kill any black for any reason; by compensating owners for a slave's maiming or death, they separated and protected all whites from all others forever. Any social ease between gentry and laborers, forged before and during that rebellion, crumbled beneath a hammer wielded in the interests of the gentry's profits.[15]

A Mercy is set during a time in American history in which racial categories were only beginning to emerge. As she presents a collection of women, all with unique backgrounds and social positions, Morrison highlights how blackness became linked not only to bondage but also to religiously based notions of evil.

Jacob is unusual among his peers in that he despises slavery. An orphan who inherited 120 acres in Dutch-held New Amsterdam from an unknown uncle, he even abhors the suffering of animals, and on his way to collect the debt owed to him by Jublio D'Ortega, a Portuguese plantation owner, he stops to free a raccoon trapped in a tree break. Jacob is disgusted by the opulence of D'Ortega's home and the obvious excess that has led to the Portuguese's substantial debt. Jacob is also aware that D'Ortega's luxurious home depends on slave labor. Despite this recognition, Jacob envies D'Ortega's house and in particular its impressive fence and gate. He imagines "a house that size on his own property," though one without D'Ortega's "pagan excess." He envisions a home that is "pure, noble even, because it would not be compromised as Jublio was" (27). The construction of this house becomes his primary obsession, as he strives to match D'Ortega's fortune without sacrificing his conscience through the abuse of others.

Despite Jacob's hatred of slavery, he agrees to take a black girl to settle D'Ortega's debt. The circumstances of this agreement are significant as the exchange refers to the mercy, a single human gesture of lasting import, mentioned in the novel's title. In response to D'Ortega's invitation to choose any of his slaves, Jacob points to the woman who served them at the dining table. D'Ortega refuses, stating that she is the main cook for his family though Jacob correctly surmises that the Portuguese is abusing her sexually. Jacob is taken aback when the slave woman, cradling a small boy on her hip, offers her daughter to him instead. She pleads, "Please, Senhor. Not me. Take her. Take my daughter" and then falls to her knees before him (26). Jacob is newly appalled at the wickedness of slavery, but prodded by D'Ortega, he agrees to take the girl. He imagines that the child, whose name is Florens, will be a welcome addition to his house, particularly by his wife, Rebekka. The two have lost three infant children to disease, and Rebekka is especially distraught over the most recent death of her only surviving daughter, Patrician.

This perplexing scene in which a mother offers her daughter to a stranger haunts Florens for the rest of her life. Cast from her mother in an act that she can only understand as rejection, Florens develops into a needy young woman, desperate for affection. She recalls how her mother held fast to her brother, suggesting a damning preference for the male child. Although Florens is the primary narrator of the novel, the final section of the book is written from the perspective of her mother and addresses Florens. It begins, "Neither one will want your brother" (162). As she addresses her daughter, this anonymous bondwoman who identifies herself only as "tua mae," Portuguese for "your mother," describes her fear of Florens's growing breasts, which threaten to attract the attention of D'Ortega and his sons (167). She explains that "To be female in this place is to be an open wound that cannot heal" and recalls how she was forced into slavery after a war devastated her family and community in Africa (163). She recalls how she was sold by black men to others whose "skin was confusing," appearing to her as either "ill or dead" (164). These European traders force her and others aboard boats destined for Barbados. Her harrowing description of the Middle Passage focuses upon her desire to commit suicide as well as the numerous rapes she endured. When they finally land, she observes how race becomes the primary determinant of her identity:

> It was there I learned how I was not a person from my country, nor from my families. I was negrita. Everything. Language, dress, gods, dance, habits, decoration, song—all of it cooked together in the color of my skin. So it was as a black that I was purchased by Senhor. (165)

Florens's mother is thus irrevocably marked by her blackness. The sign of her bondage becomes an inescapable inheritance for her two children.

Observing Jacob at D'Ortega's table, Florens's mother sees that "There was no animal in his heart. He never looked at me the way Senhor does" and most importantly when gazing at Florens he "see[s] you as a human child" (163, 166). She explains that Jacob's decision to take Florens is a mercy, a small act with enormous consequences. However, she adds that her heart will remain in the dust where she knelt before Jacob "until you understand what I know and long to tell you: to be given dominion over another is a hard thing; to wrest dominion over another is a wrong thing; to give dominion of yourself to another is a wicked thing" (167). This essential insight highlights various struggles involving slavery explored in the novel. Most importantly, it suggests that there is a key distinction between forced servitude and voluntary bondage. Florens's mother claims that there is a type of slavery that is chosen, and it is this form of enslavement which proves to be most harmful to the adolescent Florens.

After settling with D'Ortega, Jacobs takes Florens to his home in Virginia, which is occupied by Rebekka and two slave women, Lina, a Native American, and Sorrow, a largely mute African American. Despite their vastly different origins, like Jacob, all of these women are orphans. Born in London, Rebekka was sent by her parents to the New World in response to an advertisement for "a healthy, chaste wife willing to travel abroad" (74). Aware that "her prospects were servant, prostitute, wife," Rebekka welcomes the perilous journey and its uncertain outcome (77–78). Fortunately, Jacob proves to be a decent man and the two develop a loving relationship. Though Rebekka is wary of Jacob's increasing interest in expensive gifts, she is relieved when he decides to build an opulent new home because it keeps him from extended trips on the road.

Lina, however, frowns upon Jacob's new house, "which distorted sunlight and required the death of fifty trees" (43). She is certain that such unnecessary destruction will lead to misfortune, and finds the workings of Jacob, like all Europeans she has encountered, mystifying. As a child, Lina watched her entire family and tribe decimated by smallpox. After French soldiers burned her village, she was adopted by Presbyterians who named her Messalina. Fear of further abandonment leads Lina to acknowledge "her status as heathen and let herself be purified by these worthies" (47). Although Lina adapts herself to the ways of the Presbyterians—eating with utensils and giving up bathing in the river—they sell her into slavery when they discover her beaten by a man who had been her lover. At fourteen, Lina is the first person to join Jacob's household. When Rebekka arrives, the two are initially wary of one another. However, they soon become comrades, learning how to manage the farm, care for the infants, and survive the bleak, desperate winters. Lina develops her closest bond with Florens, whom she "had fallen in love with right away," as "the child assuaged the tiny yet eternal yearning for the home Lina once knew" (60). Florens delights in the attention and is especially moved by Lina's stories, in particular those "of mothers fighting to save their children" (61).

Sorrow joins Jacob's household after Rebekka but before Florens. The slave girl is discovered half dead on a riverbank by a sawyer whose wife names her Sorrow. The sawyer eventually gives her to Jacob because the latter would "do her no harm" (51). Born and raised on a ship captained by her father, Sorrow does not speak of her childhood and appears as daft and disturbed to others. She imagines that she has an identical self, which she names Twin. The two escaped together after the ship foundered. By swimming toward the horizon, they came to the shore of a river. Once rescued by the sawyer and his wife, Sorrow claims to know nothing of her past and states that mermaids and whales cast her ashore. Inept around the house, Sorrow soon gains the attention of the sawyer's two sons and is pregnant when she becomes the property of Jacob. Lina is suspicious of Sorrow's peculiar ways and keeps first Patrician and then Florens away from her. Sorrow contents herself with the company of Twin, with whom she "never wanted for friendship or conversation" (123). After helping Sorrow through the birth of her first child, Lina drowns the infant.

Sorrow is the first in the house to fall sick with the pox. Fortunately, she is cured by the blacksmith, a free black man who has been hired by Jacob to construct an intricate gate featuring two copper snakes. Jacob treats the blacksmith as "his brother," but Lina is immediately wary of his presence: "When he arrived—too shiny, way too tall, both arrogant and skilled—Lina alone saw the peril" (60). She is especially concerned by Florens's powerful response to him. The sixteen-year-old slave girl falls precipitously in love with the blacksmith, and the two have a short but passionate affair. Lina explains how she was betrayed by her lover and warns Florens against caring for a man who will inevitably return to his home without her.

After the blacksmith leaves, Jacob succumbs to the pox, dying in his empty new house. When Rebekka also becomes infected, she orders Florens to set out in search of the blacksmith, hoping that he can cure her as he did Sorrow. The novel opens with Florens traveling alone on foot to find the blacksmith. Impelled more by her love than by the mandate of her mistress, she imagines a joyous reunion with her lover. The sections of the novel narrated by Florens are addressed to her beloved. As she hurries toward the blacksmith she describes her traumatic separation from her mother and the various people she meets on her journey.

Her most significant encounter occurs when, tired and hungry, she knocks at the door of the only house lit in a small village. A woman, who introduces herself as Widow Ealing, feeds Florens and warns her that there is danger lurking. Inside the house, Florens meets the widow's daughter Jane, who has skewed eyes and bears bloody wounds on her legs. The wounds are self-inflicted, necessary to prove to religious zealots that the girl bleeds and therefore is not a demon. In the morning, the house is visited by a group of village authorities who inspect Jane's legs. However, they are soon distracted by Florens, whom they take to be "the Black Man's minion" (113). Horrified by her dark skin, they dismiss the letter penned by Rebekka attesting to her urgent errand and force her to strip off her clothes. They examine her teeth, limbs, and genitals. Florens silently endures their inspection: "Naked under their examination I watch for what is in their eyes. No hate is there or scare or disgust but they are looking at me my body across distances without recognition. Swine look at me with more connection" (113). The group leaves to discuss their findings with others and promise to return with a decision on Florens's status as human or demon. While the widow leaves to consult with the sheriff, Jane boils duck eggs for Florens and takes her to the trail that leads to the blacksmith's hamlet. Florens thanks her for her generosity, and Jane expresses her gratitude for how the slave girl provided the townspeople with a distraction from her own questionable status. When Florens asks if she is a demon, Jane replies, "Oh, yes" (114). In a world in which humans demand blood as proof of the humanity of others and dark skin signifies evil, to be a demon is to live according to other, nobler ways.

Florens at last arrives at the home of the blacksmith. Though he left without saying goodbye, he welcomes her into his small cabin. He agrees to ride back to Rebekka but insists that Florens stay because he has recently adopted a young dark-skinned boy, Malaik, whose father was found dead on his horse. Florens is determined to spend the rest of her life with the blacksmith and never return to Rebekka, but she is wary of the boy, who reminds her of her brother, the child she believes her mother loved best. The blacksmith heals Rebekka and tells Lina that Florens is safe and will return when "it suits her" (130).

Florens waits impatiently for his return, keeping her distance from Malaik, who on the second day steals her boots. In retaliation, Florens takes his doll, and as he screams, she grabs him, breaking his arm. As Malaik faints, the blacksmith enters the cabin, calling the boy's name and knocking Florens away. She understands his action as "No question. You choose the boy" (140). The blacksmith orders her to leave, refusing to hear her explanation. He states that she is a slave, but Florens does not understand:

What is your meaning? I am a slave because Sir trades for me.
No. You have become one.
How?
Your head is empty and your body is wild.
 I am adoring you.
And a slave to that too.
You alone own me.
Own yourself, woman, and leave us be. You could have killed this child.
 No. Wait. You put me in misery.
You are nothing but wilderness. No constraint. No mind.

The blacksmith's pronouncement anticipates the closing comments of Florens's mother regarding how "to give dominion of yourself to another is a wicked thing" (167). Florens is so enamored with the blacksmith that she can perceive Malaik as only a rival, not a helpless boy. Blinded by her love, she has no control over herself and no ability to care for anyone but the blacksmith. She has enslaved herself to a singular obsession and is unable to perceive herself as complete without him.

Florens returns to her former home where Sorrow has birthed another child, this time with the help of two white indentured servants, Willard and Scully. Once a mother, Sorrow renames herself Complete, suggesting that maternal love has satisfied the void that continues to haunt Florens. Complete invites Florens to escape to freedom with her, but the latter insists that she must finish her work of etching her story onto the floors and walls of Jacob's grandiose home. However, Florens implies that once finished she will burn the house: "Perhaps these words need the air that is out in the world. Need to fly up then fall, fall like ash over acres of primrose and mallow" (161). Although the destruction of Jacob's failed attempt to create a nobler version of D'Ortega's estate may signal a new physical freedom for Florens, it is the release of her long address to the blacksmith which will most liberate her. Though she has written for him, an illiterate man, Florens at last understands that her story works to free her from her destructive love; the story is her own.

Notes

1.   Kate Pickert, "Brief History Oprah's Book Club," *Time* (September 26, 2008).

2.   Caryn James, "Harnessing TV's Power to the Power of the Page," *New York Times* (November 21, 1996).

3.   Margo Jefferson, "Critic's Notebook; Writing about Race, Walking on Eggshells," *New York Times* (June 10, 1999).

4.   Elissa Schappell, "Toni Morrison: The Art of Fiction," in *Toni Morrison: Conversations*, ed. Carolyn C. Denard (Jackson, MS: University Press of Mississippi, 2008), 68.

5.   Zia Jaffrey, "Toni Morrison," in *Toni Morrison: Conversations*, ed. Carolyn C. Denard (Jackson, MS: University Press of Mississippi, 2008), 146.

6.   Carolyn C. Denard, "Blacks, Modernism, and the American South: An Interview with Toni Morrison," in *Toni Morrison: Conversations*, ed. Carolyn C. Denard (Jackson, MS: University Press of Mississippi, 2008), 190.

7.   Toni Morrison, *Paradise* (New York: Knopf, 1998), 193 (hereafter cited in text).

8.   Toni Morrison, "Home," in *The House That Race Built: Black Americans, U.S. Terrain*, ed. Waheema Lubiano (New York: Pantheon Books, 1997), 3.

9.   Ibid., 5, 9.

10.   Michiko Kakutani, "Worthy Women, Unredeemable Men," *New York Times* (January 6, 1998) and David Gates, "Review of *Paradise*," *Newsweek* (January 12, 1998).

11.   Ron David, *Toni Morrison Explained: A Reader's Road Map to the Novels* (New York: Random House, 2000), 169.

12.   Toni Morrison, *Love* (New York: Knopf, 2003), 132 (hereafter cited in text).

13.   Michiko Kakutani, "Bonds That Seem Cruel Can Be Kind," *New York Times* (November 4, 2008).

14.   Toni Morrison, "Toni Morrison Finds A Mercy in Servitude," interview by Michele Norris, NPR (October 27, 2008).

15.   Toni Morrison, *A Mercy* (New York: Knopf, 2008), 10 (hereafter cited in text).

Chapter 7

COLLABORATIONS AND CULTURAL CRITIQUES

Although Morrison is best known for her novels, she has worked in a variety of critical and artistic fields. Her commitment to African American letters has led to a wide range of endeavors including pioneering work in literary criticism, poetry, opera, cultural studies, artistic collaboration, and the promotion of black literature through popular venues, most significantly via Oprah Winfrey's Book Club. Morrison has also intervened in key national discourses that pertain to issues of race and representation. As one of the most influential artists of her generation, Morrison uses her status as a public intellectual to explore the ways in which racial categories affect individuals and ideas about national identity. Her contributions to areas outside of literary fiction demonstrate how she seeks to bridge divides between the academy and the broader social world, between art and politics, and, perhaps most importantly, between theory and daily life.

Playing in the Dark: Whiteness and the Literary Imagination was published in 1992 but is based on the William E. Massey Sr. Lectures in the History of American Civilization that Morrison delivered at Harvard University in 1990. The central ideas of this slim but extremely influential book were also the foundation for a course in American literature that Morrison taught at Princeton. In the three essays collected in *Playing in the Dark*,

Morrison highlights how literature nurtures and reflects national ideologies. The American canon exposes foundational values, anxieties, and aspirations that have significant political import. Morrison begins by asserting that existing literary criticism has occluded the ways in which traditional conceptions of American identity depend on an "Africanist presence." Building upon the ideas expressed in her 1988 Tanner Lecture on Human Values at the University of Michigan, which was later published in the *Michigan Quarterly Review* as "Unspeakable Things Unspoken: The Afro-American Presence in American Literature," Morrison reads canonical American writers attentive to how blackness functions as a necessary foil to a manufactured notion of whiteness.

In the opening essay, "Black Matters," Morrison describes how being an African American woman writer influences her approach to reading, allowing her to understand the ways in which language shapes racial identities. Frustrated with an approach to American literature that assumes that the canon is uninfluenced by "the four-hundred-year-old presence of, first, Africans and then African-Americans in the United States," she contends that "the major and championed characteristics of our national literature—individualism, masculinity, social engagement versus historical isolation; acute and ambiguous moral problematics; the thematics of innocence coupled with an obsession with figurations of death and hell" are "responses to a dark, abiding, signing Africanist presence."[1]

Morrison explains that an Africanist presence is not unique to the literature of the United States but is evident in the works of other countries. However, she notes that while nations in Europe and South America have begun to explore the implications of racialized discourse, such discussions have failed to emerge in the United States. American literary criticism has avoided exploring how representations of blackness and black characters operate to create both implicit and explicit racial hierarchies. Referencing texts by Henry James, Ernest Hemingway, William Faulkner, and Flannery O'Connor, Morrison claims that "the literature of the United States has taken as its concern the architecture of a *new white man*" (14–15). However, this conception of rugged individuality depends on the fabrication of an Africanist persona that reflects not the reality of black people, but the desires and anxieties of its white creators.

Morrison then proceeds to do a close reading of Willa Cather's last novel, *Sapphira and the Slave Girl* (1940), a text that has largely been dismissed or ignored by critics. Morrison understands this oversight as a refusal by scholars to engage in the central concern of the text, specifically, the ways in which white female identity depends on the abjection of black bondwomen. She notes that the novel's title establishes the racialized hierarchy evident throughout the text as Nancy, the slave girl, is robbed of an individual identity. Morrison exposes the illogic of Cather's plot, which involves the machinations of Sapphira, an invalid who believes her husband is sexually attracted to Nancy, the adolescent daughter of her most devoted female slave, Till. Sapphira invites her lecherous nephew Martin to visit with the hope that he will rape Nancy and consequently Sapphira will regain her husband's full attention. Morrison notes that sexual activity between Nancy and Martin would hardly make the former any less attractive to Sapphira's husband and questions the integrity of Cather's description of Till, who aids her mistress in executing the planned rape of her daughter. Nancy decides to escape only at the urging of Sapphira's abolitionist daughter Rachel, revealing the paucity of imagination and intellect Cather affords black characters. Morrison concludes, "These fictional demands stretch to breaking all narrative coherence" (23). However, such obvious disruptions highlight how Sapphira's identity and power depends on the degradation of her young and sexually attractive slave girl. The needs and desires of the white mistress take precedence over narrative coherence and the presentation of realistic black characters.

The second essay in *Playing in the Dark*, "Romancing the Shadow," opens with a passage from Edgar Allan Poe's *The Narrative of Arthur Gordon Pym* (1838), which describes the appearance of a white giant to a band of sailing castaways. Morrison cites Poe's work as an example of "figurations of impenetrable whiteness that surface in American literature whenever an Africanist presence is engaged" (32–33). She reads them as symbols of power that contrast with the impotence and subservience accorded to accompanying images of blackness. American identity depends on the promise of freedom, which has been constructed as a universal longing for its enterprising new citizens. The American Dream presumes a flight from oppression and the embrace of a limitless future.

However, this vision exploited what Herman Melville called "the power of blackness," a slave population that Morrison claims was used "as surrogate selves for meditation on problems of human freedom, its lure and elusiveness" (37). Freedom became meaningful only in opposition to slavery and to the blackness that defined those held in bondage. Morrison asserts:

> Black slavery enriched the country's creative possibilities. For in that construction of blackness and enslavement could be found not only the not-free but also, with the dramatic polarity created by skin color, the projection of the not-me. (38)

Citing Emerson's essay "The American Scholar" and *Voyagers to the West* (1986), Bernard Bailyn's historical account of European settlers in the United States, Morrison demonstrates how American identity was constituted not only as white and male but also as intimately linked to a notion of freedom as dominion over others.

Morrison further contends that American identity is figured as fundamentally innocent, that the newness of the frontier and its inhabitants translates as an escape from certain historical realities and histories. She points to the stark contradiction between a democratic country premised on individual freedom and the enforced bondage of its black population. Any discourse about the fledgling nation must have in some way addressed this obvious paradox even if the language used was coded rather than explicit in its reference of Africans and their descendants.

In order to explore the nature of this silence and disavowal, Morrison proposes a series of topics for critical investigation. She urges examination of how the Africanist character works as a surrogate and guardian of celebrated American qualities. The use of an Africanist idiom—that is, the dialogue of black characters—must also be studied to understand how such language enforces power hierarchies and social difference. She also highlights the need for investigation of literary techniques used to "enforce the invention and implications of whiteness," such as how the sexuality and vulnerability of black characters reflect upon white counterparts (52). Finally, Morrison calls for the analysis of Africanist narrative as reflections on one's own humanity, that is, how the stories of blacks were appropriated to support prevailing national ideologies. She ends this chapter by briefly taking up Mark Twain's *The Adventures of Huckleberry Finn* and returning to images of whiteness in Poe's works to demonstrate the urgency of her proposed project. Both examples indicate the dependence of white freedom on black enslavement and point to the necessity of applying this critical approach to additional authors like William Faulkner and Saul Bellow.

Morrison begins "Disturbing Nurses and the Kindness of Sharks," the book's final essay, by stating, "Race has become metaphorical—a way of referring to and disguising forces, events, classes, and expressions of social decay and economic division far more threatening to the body politic than biological 'race' ever was" (63). Racial categorization is a means of establishing hierarchical difference. In this way, race provides a vocabulary that both enforces and occludes difference by relying upon false claims of biological difference. Morrison argues that Africanism has evolved through American literature. It was first used to express rigid hierarchical categories but has become a tool to express metaphysical anxieties and forbidden desires.

By approaching texts attentive to Africanist constructions, Morrison notes that it is possible to generate oppositional readings, that is, to discern subtexts that contradict surface meanings. This complexity demands further study of how Africanist images operate. Morrison lists six linguistic strategies that capitalize upon Africanist assumptions: (1) the use of concise stereotypes that depend on racist assumptions; (2) metonyms, such as color and physical traits, that encode prejudice; (3) metaphysical condensation such as referring to certain groups as animal-like; (4) fetishization to invoke false differences such as race-specific blood; (5) dehistoricizing allegory that universalizes difference; and (6) patterns of fragmented and repetitive language that are associated to specific characters or ideas rather than to an instability in the text itself.

Having described these strategies in brief detail, Morrison then applies them in her analysis of Hemingway's work. She cites Hemingway's depiction of a black crew member named Wesley in *To Have and Have Not* (1937), noting the text's strained syntax in order to deny the black man agency and power. By referring to Wesley as "the nigger," the protagonist Harry refuses him both specificity and humanity. Yet without this foil, Morrison argues that Harry would "lack the complimentarity of a figure who can be assumed to be in some way bound, fixed, unfree, and serviceable," all that Harry is not (91). When Wesley speaks it is only to articulate grumbles and complaints that demonstrate his weakness in comparison to Harry's strength and stoicism.

Morrison elaborates upon this discussion by also describing how an Africanist presence functions in Hemingway's depiction of relationships between men and women. She cites a passage again from *To Have and Have Not* in which Marie, Harry's wife, fondly recalls her husband's sexuality and power. Marie describes an encounter in which Harry smacked a "nigger" who said something to her. She laughs at Harry's bold response and then segues into a description of having her hair dyed blonde for the first time. Morrison argues that these two scenes are connected, claiming that threatened by the ease with which "the nigger" approached her, Marie must establish her whiteness in no uncertain terms. She is transformed by her new hair and becomes instantly attractive to Harry.

Morrison concludes her discussion of Hemingway's work by citing a conversation between Harry and Marie. Marie asks Harry if he ever had sex with a black woman, in her words, "a nigger wench." Harry replies that he has, describing the sex as "like nurse shark" (85). Harry perceives black women so beyond the realm of human as to be fish. Morrison reads this astounding comment alongside Hemingway's previous representations of nurses as tender, caring women. These protective nurses are typically juxtaposed against opposing figures, "the devouring predator whose inhuman and indifferent impulses posed immediate danger" (84). Morrison observes that in Hemingway's fiction, black men are often used to express impending doom, while women like Mrs. Macomber in "The Short Happy Life of Francis Macomber" actually destroy their mates. Thus the phrase "nurse shark" fuses the predatory animal with the facade of a nurturing figure.

Morrison ends *Playing in the Dark* by stating that her literary analysis is not meant as a study of the racial attitudes of particular authors. Her concern is not with biography but with literary representations. Although judgments about certain authors may be made, she is not interested in delineating between racist and nonracist literature. She explains: "My project is an effort to avert the critical gaze from the racial object to the racial subject; from the described and imagined to the describers and imaginers; from the serving to the served" (90).

Morrison acknowledges the power of Hemingway's fiction to describe an experience of white American masculinity and insists that further criticism should examine all aspects of such gendered foundations, including the "disrupting darkness before its eyes" (91).

Since the publication of *Playing in the Dark,* many scholars have responded to this call to examine the Africanist presence in American literature, and as Morrison has noted in more recent publications, race is now a common subject of discussion in academic circles. *Playing in the Dark* is required reading for graduate students in English and other affiliated disciplines. The American literary canon is no longer understood as simply a catalog of great works. Rather, scholars continue to explore how the canon has contributed to a certain conception of American identity as largely white, male, and free while pushing to expand what constitutes American literature.

Morrison's concern for how such master narratives, that is, accepted conceptions of national identity, are constructed has extended beyond the realm of literary fiction to consider significant recent social events. All of the political issues upon which she has chosen to comment—the Anita Hill and Clarence Thomas hearing, the O.J. Simpson case, President Clinton's sex scandal with Monica Lewinsky, and Barack Obama's presidential run—highlight her contention that "the site of the exorcism of critical national issues was situated in the miasma of black life and inscribed on the bodies of black people."[2] According to Morrison, just as an Africanist presence works in American literary texts to provide support for a white national identity, public scandals most often use black bodies to express anxieties about social relationships.

In 1992, Morrison edited *Race-ing Justice, En-Gendering Power: Essays on Anita Hill, Clarence Thomas, and the Construction of Social Reality,* a collection of essays on the Supreme Court justice's controversial appointment. In her introduction, "Friday on the Potomac," Morrison draws attention to how Clarence Thomas was frequently described in the national media with reference to his body. She argues that by focusing on his laugh or his penchant for weight lifting, journalists reified long-standing associations of African Americans with the physical while also minimizing his intellectual achievements and capabilities. This attention to Thomas's body became fully realized once Anita Hill voiced her accusations of sexual misconduct. Morrison argues that such damning claims would have eliminated a white nominee immediately, but given the race of both the accuser and the accused, Hill's testimony became an occasion for the nation to showcase its concerns about "male prerogative and sexual assault, the issues of racial justice and racial redress, the problematics of governing and controlling women's bodies, the alterations of work space into (sexually) domesticated space . . . upon the canvas/flesh of black people" (xix–xx).

In her most damning critique, Morrison likens Thomas to the Indian servant Friday from Daniel Defoe's 1719 adventure tale *Robinson Crusoe*. In the novel, Friday is described as a "savage cannibal" who after being saved by Crusoe becomes civilized and Christianized through the white man's studious efforts.[3] Morrison notes that according to Crusoe, Friday had no language and though he misses his home, he pledges to always serve and obey his white master. Friday symbolically places Crusoe's foot upon his head to indicate his devotion. After briefly describing Thomas's rise in the political sphere and his rather indifferent approach to combating racism, Morrison concludes: "the language he speaks, the actions he takes, the Supreme Court decisions he has made or aligned himself with, the foot, as it were, that he has picked up and placed on his head, give us some indication of what his choice has been" (xxix).

Despite Morrison's obvious dissatisfaction with the nature of the hearings as well as the ultimate confirmation of Thomas to the Supreme Court, she lauds the fact that "In matters of race and gender, it is now possible and necessary, as it seemed never to have been before, to speak about these matters without the barriers, the silences, the embarrassing gaps in discourse." The very fact that Hill contested Thomas's nomination demonstrates that African Americans cannot be treated as a monolithic political or social force. Morrison thus takes this occasion to provide "thoughtful, incisive, and far-ranging dialogue" on the hearings that might elucidate its meaning and implications for all of American society (xxx). The contributors to the intellectual exchange established in *Race-ing Justice, En-Gendering Power* include numerous prominent law and political science professors such as Kimberlé Crenshaw and Manning Marable as well as cultural theorists like Homi K. Bhabha, Wahneema Lubiano, and Cornel West.

Although many critics disagreed with Morrison's contention that Thomas rejected his black identity in order to succeed in white America, the publication of this book along with her growing popularity as a novelist propelled her into the national spotlight. She became a major public figure, offering strong opinions on issues as diverse as the 1992 Los Angeles riots and the aftermath of 9/11. Moreover, Morrison demonstrated how literary texts like *Robinson Crusoe* could be usefully applied to contemporary social and political dynamics. She drew upon this same model of analysis and collective dialogue five years later in the edited collection *Birth of a Nation'hood: Gaze, Script and Spectacle in the O.J. Simpson Case*.

Throughout the summer of 1994, the country was riveted by the murder trial of former football star and actor O.J. Simpson. In June, Simpson's ex-wife Nicole Brown Simpson and her friend Ronald Goldman were found fatally stabbed outside Brown's condominium in Brentwood, California. Early evidence pointed to Simpson, and the Los Angeles police department agreed to allow Simpson to turn himself in a few days after the murder. However, when Simpson did not appear, an all-points bulletin was released, leading to the infamous low-speed chase of Simpson's white Ford Bronco that eventually led to his surrender. The ensuing criminal trial only heightened the sense of spectacle established by this opening episode. Court TV televised the entire proceeding and the nation watched transfixed, debating the evidence against the former football star.

Appalled by the public frenzy generated by the trial and the often gross racism apparent in the media (*Time* magazine ran a cover photo of Simpson's mug shot which had been darkened to make his complexion blacker than it actually was), Morrison worked with Princeton professor Claudia Brodsky Lacour to compile a collection of essays analyzing the Simpson spectacle and its import from a range of disciplinary perspectives. With contributions from such prominent intellectuals as law professor Patricia Williams, Chief Judge Emeritus A. Leon Higginbotham, and novelist Ishmael Reed, the collection explores how the Simpson trial reveals lasting social tensions in American society from various historical, legal, psychological, and linguistic approaches.

Morrison opens *Birth of a Nation'hood* with a powerful introduction that links Simpson's media treatment to Herman Melville's short story

"Benito Cereno." In this masterful tale, Captain Delano, a well-intentioned but deeply racist American, boards the San Dominick, a distressed ship whose captain, Benito Cereno, seems inexplicably aloof and anxious. Delano looks upon the African slaves in tow as docile animals and is especially taken by the obsequious Babo, Cereno's personal servant. Blinded by his belief in the inferiority of blacks, Delano is unable to see that in fact the slaves, having executed a successful revolt, are in full control of the ship and are only performing expected racial roles.

Morrison draws attention to how easily Delano shifts his perception of the Africans—from natural servants to violent brutes—once he is made aware of the true state of affairs aboard the San Dominick, a remarkable transformation that reflects the media's depiction of O.J. Simpson:

> Like the readers of Herman Melville's "Benito Cereno," contemporary "readers" of the Simpson case have been encouraged to move from a previous assessment of Mr. Simpson as an affable athlete/spokesperson to a judgment of him as a wild dog. He clearly is, according to mainstream wisdom, the latter. And the wild dog portrait layered over him contains a further incompatibility: cool, cunning, even intelligent malfeasance or raging, mindless, brutal insanity. The language developing around him portrays a thoughtful, meditating murderer capable of slick and icy-cold deliberations *and/or* mindless, spontaneous killer—a kind of lucky buffoon. That each cluster of adjectives cancels out the other is of no moment since contradiction, incoherence and emotional disorder "fit" when the subject is black.[4]

The wild shift in perception that Morrison observes in the media's treatment of Simpson demonstrates how the black body has perpetually acted as a site of contradiction and illogic. Simpson's alleged crime need not make sense because the actions of a black man do not require reason; violence and disorder are expected outcomes. Although many of the essays in the collection do not take up the issue of Simpson's actual guilt or innocence, instead focusing upon the ways in which he was represented by the media, Morrison has stated that she is wholly convinced of his innocence.[5]

This is not the only controversial stance Morrison has taken on national affairs. In 1998, she published a widely discussed article in the *New Yorker* in which she comments on President Clinton's sexual affair with White House intern Monica Lewinsky. Tired of the dizzying twenty-four-hour news cycle, which broadcasted opinions of professors, prosecutors, consultants, and other seeming experts, Morrison opted "to get my news the old-fashioned way: conversation, public eavesdropping, and word of mouth."[6] Her hope was to discover the meaning behind the media spectacle that had driven journalists into a frenzy and left the public stunned with unseemly intimate details. Dismissing claims that the Clinton scandal was fundamentally about adultery or even high crimes, Morrison argues that "what the public has been given is dangerously close to a story of no story at all," a consequence of "the absence of a coherent sphere of enunciation."[7] She cites the contradictory discourses that emerged from the scandal as it became an occasion for gossip and sermonizing, for comedy and lessons on morality.

In her attempt to make sense of this welter of language, Morrison turns to the perspective of African American men, who she claims "seemed to understand it right away." Even before the Lewinsky scandal, when the Clintons were being investigated for their partnership in the Whitewater Development Corporation, Morrison claims black men said that "white skin notwithstanding, this is our first black President." To support this bold contention, Morrison does not rely upon a biological definition of race but instead points to social traits that link Clinton to African American identity. She explains:

> Clinton displays almost every trope of blackness: single-parent household, born poor, working-class, saxophone-playing, McDonald's-and-junk-food-loving boy from Arkansas. And when virtually all the African-American Clinton appointees began, one by one, to disappear, when the President's body, his privacy, his unpoliced sexuality became the focus of the persecution, when he was metaphorically seized and bodysearched, who could gainsay these black men who knew whereof they spoke?[8]

Morrison saw in the media's treatment of Clinton the same assumption of guilt that drove journalists to condemn O.J. Simpson; both represent the "always and already guilty 'perp,'" a figure of blackness who is denied the presumption of innocence and whose sexual life may be freely exposed.[9] This is the same Africanist figure from *Playing in the Dark*, the black body that is hopelessly corrupt, already born into guilt. From Morrison's perspective, Clinton's white skin is irrelevant to the damning treatment he received by the media. He was treated as a black man by being converted into a sexualized spectacle for the public's titillation.

Morrison was roundly criticized for her comments. Many found her claim about Clinton's blackness to validate damaging racial stereotypes. Others contended that her essay undermined the history of demonization African American men have suffered. While black men have been lynched and beaten throughout the nineteenth and twentieth centuries for no cause other than the color of their skin, Clinton was guilty of placing himself in compromising positions with Monica Lewinsky. Perhaps most disturbing was her statement that Clinton was "Blacker than any actual black person who could ever be elected in our children's lifetime."[10] Not only would this claim be wholly disproved a mere ten years later with the election of Barack Obama, but her comment stung with hopelessness regarding the possibilities of black achievement.

Nonetheless, Morrison's characterization of Clinton as the nation's first black president had remarkable staying power. In 2001, the Congressional Black Caucus celebrated the former president at its Annual Awards Dinner in Washington DC. Representative Eddie Bernice Johnson of Texas told the audience that Clinton "took so many initiatives he made us think for a while we had elected the first black president."[11] During his presidential campaign, Obama was asked if he agreed with Morrison's contention that Clinton was the first black president. He responded first by acknowledging Clinton's "enormous affinity with the African-American community" but then added, "I would have to investigate more Bill's dancing abilities and some of this other stuff before I accurately judged whether he was, in fact, a brother."[12] Obama, more than most, understood Morrison's recognition of the malleable meanings attached to race. Though many were startled by Morrison's assertion concerning President Clinton's blackness, as early as 1987, she expressed her belief in the ability of individuals to select their racial identification:

Now people choose their identities. Now people choose to be Black. They used to be born Black. That's not true anymore. You can be Black genetically and choose not to be. You just change your mind or your eyes, change anything. It's just a mind-set.[13]

Morrison here describes that choice in racial identification is a new phenomenon, suggesting that race, like culture and political ideology, is subject to individual inclinations. This radical formulation points to the fluid nature of both identity and community.

In 2008, Morrison issued a letter to various news sources endorsing Senator Barack Obama for president. Obama was in the midst of a fierce campaign for the Democratic nomination, struggling against front-runner Senator Hillary Clinton. He contacted Morrison to ask for her support, first noting his deep admiration for *Song of Solomon*. She had been especially impressed by Obama's first book, *Dreams from My Father: A Story of Race and Inheritance* (1995), which describes his adolescent struggles with family and identity as well as his experiences as a community organizer in Chicago. Commenting on his book, she has stated, "I was astonished by his ability to write, to think, to reflect, to learn and turn a good phrase. I was very impressed. This was not a normal political biography."[14]

In her public letter to Obama, Morrison explains that this marks her first public endorsement of a presidential candidate. Given the country's fraught political landscape—ongoing wars in Iraq and Afghanistan, impending signs of economic collapse, the fallout from Hurricane Katrina, and continued dissatisfaction with America's international reputation— she felt compelled to voice support for his candidacy. She acknowledges her admiration for Senator Clinton and affirms that she is making her endorsement not due to considerations of race or gender. Rather, in her estimation, Senator Obama exhibits exceptional qualities of mind and special talents. Addressing him directly, she writes that "in addition to keen intelligence, integrity and a rare authenticity, you exhibit something that has nothing to do with age, experience, race or gender and something I don't see in other candidates. That something is a creative imagination which coupled with brilliance equals wisdom."[15]

Morrison was too anxious to watch the election results that November. She was notified by phone about Obama's victory because her computer crashed and her television was not working. Describing her response to Obama's historic win, Morrison said, "I felt this relief like something was lifted . . . It made me feel like that phrase Martin Luther King Jr. had said about being to the mountaintop. I could never visualize the metaphor until now."[16] Morrison also praised the country's active reinvention of itself, its dynamic exploration of democracy and identity through the election of Obama, and suggested that were Ralph Ellison alive he would have to re-title his masterpiece *Visible Man*. She also noted that Obama's victory could pave the way for dramatic shifts in race relations all over the globe.

While Morrison has most often focused her attention on matters of serious national and literary concern, she has also experimented with lighter artistic forms. In 1999, she began a literary partnership with her son Slade, a graphic artist. The two coauthored *The Big Box*, a children's book based on a story that Slade devised when he was nine. Written in rhyme, *The Big Box* describes three rebellious children, Patty, Mickey, and Sue, who are sent to the big box when they do things like talk in the library and have too much fun, activities that make the grown-ups nervous. They tell the children: "We all agree, your parents and we,/That you simply can't handle your freedom." The big box is full of toys and treats but lacks any connection to the natural world. The aquarium has plastic fish, and there is a picture of the sky hanging on the wall. Most significantly, however, "the door only opens one way." The children, aware of the false paradise offered by the big box, comment to the adults, "If freedom is handled just your way/Then it's not my freedom or free."[17]

The Big Box, vividly illustrated by Giselle Potter, revisits many of the key themes of Morrison's work including the nature of freedom and the importance of transgression. While these ideas clearly resonate with readers of Morrison's fiction, many found *The Big Box* to be overly didactic and clumsy in its verse, a book with greater appeal to adults than children. Despite this disappointing response, Morrison continued writing children's books with Slade. They published *The Book of Mean People* in 2002, a story about a child who insists on smiling and being himself despite the disapproval of others. In 2003, they began work on a series of books called *Who's Got Game?* In these clever revisions of Aesop's fables, the two Morrisons update the original stories, sometimes changing the ending or providing more complex character-izations. The books are richly illustrated in comic book form by Pascal LeMaitre. There are four books in the series: *The Ant or the Grasshopper?* (2003), *The Lion or the Mouse?* (2003), *Poppy or the Snake?* (2004), and *The Mirror or the Glass?* (2007).

Morrison has written one book for children on her own, *Remember: The Journey to School Integration* (2004). As with *The Black Book*, Morrison here gathers historical photographs about black life, though in this collection all of the pictures are concerned with the process of desegregation as mandated by the *Brown v. Board of Education* decision. In the introduction, Morrison writes to her audience of young readers:

> This book is about you. Even though the main event in the story took place many years ago, what happened before it and after it is now part of all our lives. Because remembering is the mind's first step toward understanding, this book is designed to take you on a journey through a time in American life when there was as much hate as there was love; as much anger as there was hope; as many heroes as cowards.[18]

Dedicated to the four girls who died in the bombing of a Birmingham church in 1963, the book asks readers to understand their own lives through the struggle and hope of others. Freedom as we experience it now only exists because of the sacrifice and leadership of previous generations.

In addition to working with her son creatively, throughout the 1990s Morrison worked closely with Andre Previn and Kathleen Battle, writing lyrics for various musical pieces. These collaborative experiences required Morrison to think of language in new ways, as a supplement to music and dramatic performances. She enjoyed this approach to artistic development so much that she decided to duplicate the process by setting up the Princeton Atelier. Founded in 2004, this studio arts program invites artists from various genres to work with Princeton students and faculty from all disciplines to develop collaborative artistic productions. Atelier courses culminate in a final public presentation of the work. Guest artists have included choreographer Jacques d'Amboise, vocal group Anonymous 4, cellist Yo-Yo Ma, novelist Gabriel García

Márquez, visual artist Irina Nakhova, the Pig Iron Theatre Company, Bernice Johnson Reagon of Sweet Honey in the Rock, and theater director Peter Sellars. Princeton faculty members, including Joyce Carol Oates, Peter Jeffery, Steve Mackey, and Michael Cadden, have also led classes at the Atelier. Morrison now works as a consultant to the program, having handed the directorship to poet and chair of the Lewis Center for the Arts Paul Muldoon.

Beyond the Atelier, Morrison has explored her writing in other forms of artistic collaboration. In 2003, she published *Five Poems,* a short collection of poetry with illustrations by African American graphic artist Kara Walker. Only 425 copies of *Five Poems* were issued by Rainmaker Editions of Las Vegas, and because the book does not have an international standard book number, few critics even know of its existence. Published after the completion of the trilogy novels, *Five Poems* demonstrates continued engagement with the themes and ideas at the forefront of those texts: love, mortality, transgression, memory, and the complex relationship between women and desire. The poems draw upon a network of images explored throughout the trilogy, linking scenes from the three novels in unexpected and elucidating ways. For example, the second poem, "The Perfect Ease of Grain," references the scene in *Beloved* in which Halle and Sethe have sex for the first time. The poem contrasts the bounty of harvest with the longing caused by a woman. In the final stanza, the opening two lines, "The perfect ease of grain/Time enough to spill," are repeated but the line "The flavor of a woman carried through the rain" is replaced with "The flavor of a woman remembered on a train."[19] The image of the train shifts the poem out of the historical context of antebellum slavery and into a more contemporary environment, which anticipates the setting of *Jazz.*

Of particular significance to *Five Poems* is how Morrison develops and expands upon her representation of Beloved. While critics continue to argue about who she is and what she represents, the rampant and varied allusions to *Beloved* in the poems attest to the dynamic potential of this key literary figure. Moreover, by linking Beloved to both the biblical Eve and the ancient scriptural manuscript "Thunder, Perfect Mind," Morrison presents her as an entity of lasting divine import who may be understood as a type of ancestral presence. The loosely related poems of her collection envision the possibilities of an ancestor based on many of the characteristics evident in Beloved—an ancestor strongly correlated to the return of memory, a woman who embodies oppositions and possesses multiple meanings, and a figure of transgressive female power. By tracing a line of descent from Eve to Beloved, Morrison reconfigures our understanding of the original female ancestor as a divine immortal presence.

Although well into her seventies, Morrison continues to develop new projects that provide opportunities for people to come together and talk about art and history. In 2006, she accepted an invitation from the Louvre Museum in Paris to lead a conversation on a theme of her choice. Morrison selected "The Foreigner's Home" and helped design a multidisciplinary exploration of exile, immigration, and displacement. A wide range of artists and curators joined Morrison to examine these ideas through various artistic mediums. With graphite attached to his hands and feet, choreographer William Forsythe performed a solo dance on a sheet of white paper that was inspired by Francis Bacon's last portrait. The graphite left marks on the paper, creating a drawing based on the interpretation of another drawing. "The Foreigner's Home" also included film screenings, mapped routes through the Louvre that highlighted pieces which involve immigration and exile, as well as a public dialogue between Morrison and writers Edwige Danticat, Michael Ondaatje, and Boubacar Boris Diop.

Most recently Morrison edited *Burn This Book: PEN Writers Speak Out on the Power of the Word*, which was published in 2009 in conjunction with the PEN American Center. Dedicated to protecting free expression around the world, PEN is the oldest ongoing human rights organization. The eleven essays collected in *Burn This Book*, from such writers as Salman Rushdie, Orhan Pamuk, and Nadine Gordimer, examine the consequences of censorship and testify to the importance of literature to enhance our understanding and experience of the world. This collection is notable for its global approach to issues of free speech and the literary marketplace, demonstrating a new commitment on the part of Morrison to move beyond specifically American concerns. In her opening essay, titled "Peril," Morrison describes how parallel to the history of literature is the development of techniques to censor the work of writers. She explains that "it is imperative not only to save the besieged writers but to save ourselves" because all writers contribute to "sharpening the moral imagination."[20] She concludes, "A writer's life and work are not a gift to mankind. They are its necessity."[21]

Morrison's legacy has also found physical embodiment in the Bench by the Road Project, which is sponsored by the Toni Morrison Society, a nonprofit organization of scholars and readers of Morrison's work. Morrison wrote *Beloved* in part because there was no physical monument to American slavery, "no bench by the road" to commemorate those who suffered, died, and survived:

> There is no place you or I can go, to think about or not think about, to summon the presence of, or recollect the absences of slaves; nothing that reminds us of the ones who made the journey and of those who did not make it. There is no suitable memorial or plaque or wreath or wall or park or skyscraper lobby. There's no three-hundred-foot tower. There's no small bench by the road . . . And because such a place doesn't exist (that I know of), the book had to.[22]

In the summer of 2008 Morrison finally sat on that "bench by the road" on Sullivan's Island off the South Carolina coast. The six-foot-long, twenty-six-inch-deep black steel bench was built with help from the National Park Service and the Toni Morrison Society. The site was chosen because Sullivan's Island is home to Fort Moultrie, which was a point of entry for approximately 40 percent of the Africans who were enslaved in the United States. The bench at Sullivan's Island is the first of a series of ten benches that will be placed at locations significant to African American history and in many cases featured in Morrison's fiction. They include Fifth Avenue in Harlem, the site of Emmett Till's murder in Mississippi, and an Underground Railroad site in Oberlin, Ohio, near Morrison's hometown of Lorain.

Attending the dedication ceremony for the bench, Morrison reflected, "It's never too late to honor the dead. It's never too late to applaud the living who do them honor."[23] Morrison sat on the bench that she envisioned first through words—history at last made physical through her commitment to language and the memory of African American lives. The bench is only one example of the transformative power of her writing and the ways in which she has influenced numerous aspects of American life. The benches, like her novels, are for all people. They are sites to contemplate the past, the complexities of human nature, and the stories that teach us who we are.

Notes

1. Toni Morrison, *Playing in the Dark: Whiteness and the Literary Imagination* (Cambridge, MA: Harvard University Press, 1992), 5 (hereafter cited in text).

2. Toni Morrison, "Introduction: Friday on the Potomac," in *Race-ing Justice, En-Gendering Power: Essays on Anita Hill, Clarence Thomas, and the Construction of Social Reality*, ed. Toni Morrison (New York: Pantheon, 1992), x (hereafter cited in text).

3. Daniel Defoe, *Robinson Crusoe* (Whitefish, MT: Kessinger Publishing, 2004), 83.

4. Toni Morrison, "The Official Story: Dead Man Golfing," in *Birth of a Nation'hood: Gaze, Script and Spectacle in the O.J. Simpson Case*, eds. Toni Morrison and Claudia Brodsky Lacour (New York: Pantheon, 1997), viii-ix.

5. Zia Jaffrey, "Toni Morrison," in *Toni Morrison: Conversations*, ed. Carolyn C. Denard (Jackson, MS: University Press of Mississippi, 2008), 148.

6. Toni Morrison, "Talk of the Town," in *What Moves at the Margin: Selected Nonfiction*, ed. Carolyn C. Denard (Jackson, MS: University Press of Mississippi, 2008), 149.

7. Ibid., 151.

8. Ibid., 152.

9. Ibid., 153.

10. Ibid., 152.

11. Qtd. in George Curry, "Bill Clinton: Pimp Daddy President," *The Washington Informer* (January 31, 2008).

12. Qtd. in Kevin Connolly, "Struggle for the African American Vote," *BBC News* (January 23, 2008).

13. Elsie B. Washington, "Talk with Toni Morrison," in *Conversations with Toni Morrison*, ed. Danille Taylor-Guthrie (Jackson, MS: University Press of Mississippi, 1994), 236.

14. "Toni Morrison Talks Obama," *EURWeb.Com* (November 7, 2008).

15. Toni Morrison, "Letter to Obama," http://firstread.msnbc.msn.com/archive/2008/01/28/614795.aspx.

16.   Jamin Brophy-Warren, "A Writer's Vote," *The Wall Street Journal* (November 7, 2008).

17.   Toni Morrison and Slade Morrison, *The Big Box* (New York: Hyperion, 1999).

18.   Toni Morrison, *Remember: The Journey to School Integration* (Boston: Houghton, 2004), 3.

19.   Toni Morrison, *Five Poems* (Las Vegas, NV: Rainmaker Editions, 2002).

20.   Toni Morrison, "Peril," in *Burn This Book: PEN Writers Speak Out on the Power of the Word*, ed. Toni Morrison (New York: HarperStudio, 2009), 3-4.

21.   Ibid., 4.

22.   Toni Morrison, "A Bench by the Road: Beloved," in *Toni Morrison: Conversations*, ed. Carolyn C. Denard (Jackson, MS: University Press of Mississippi, 2008), 44.

23.   Felicia Lee, "Bench of Memory at Slavery's Gateway," *New York Times* (July 28, 2008).

SELECTED BIBLIOGRAPHY

Primary Sources

Morrison, Toni. "Banquet Speech." Nobelprize.org (December 10, 1993). http://nobelprize.org/nobel_prizes/literature/laureates/1993/morrison-speech.html.

———. "Behind the Making of *The Black Book*." *Black World* 23 (February 1974): 86–90.

———. *Beloved*. New York: A.A. Knopf, 1987.

———. "A Bench by the Road." With Robert Richardson. [*Unitarian Universalist*] *World* 3.1 (Jan.–Feb. 1989): 4+.

———, ed. *The Black Book*. Comp. Middleton Harris et al. New York: Random, 1974.

———. *The Bluest Eye*. New York: Holt, 1970.

———, ed. *Burn This Book: PEN Writers Speak Out on the Power of the Word*. New York: Harper Studio, 2009.

———. *The Dancing Mind: Speech upon Acceptance of the National Book Foundation Medal for Distinguished Contribution to American Letters*. New York: Knopf, 1996.

———. "The Dead of September 11." *Vanity Fair*, November 2001.

———. "The Family Came First." Review of *Labor of Love, Labor of Sorrow*, by Jacqueline Jones. *New York Times Book Review*, 14 April 1985.

———. "The Fisherwoman: Introduction to *A Kind of Rapture: Photographs*." In *A Kind of Rapture: Photographs by Robert Bergman*, i–iv. New York: Pantheon, 1998.

———. *Five Poems*. Las Vegas, NV: Rainmaker Editions, 2002.

———. "For a Heroic Writers Movement." *Political Affairs* 60, no. 12 (December 1981): 14–17.

———. "Foreword to *The Harlem Book of the Dead*." In *The Harlem Book of the Dead* by James Van Der Zee, Owen Dodson, and Camille Billops. Dobbs Ferry, NY: Morgan and Morgan, 1978.

———. "Foreword to *Writing Red: An Anthology of American Women Writers, 1930–1940*." In *Writing Red: An Anthology of American Women Writers, 1930–1940*, edited by Charlotte Nekola and Paula Rabinowitz, ix–x. New York: Feminist Press at CUNY, 1987.

———. "Going Home with Bitterness and Joy." Review of *South to a Very Old Place*, by Albert Murray. *New York Times Book Review*, 2 January 1972.

———. "Home." In *The House That Race Built: Black Americans, U.S. Terrain*, edited by Wahneema Lubiano, 3–12. New York: Pantheon, 1997.

———. "How Can Values Be Taught in the University?" *Michigan Quarterly Review* 40, no. 2 (2001): 273–78.

———. "Introduction." In Mark Twain, *The Adventures of Huckleberry Finn*. New York: Oxford University Press, 1996.

———. "Introduction." In Camara Laye, *The Radiance of the King*, trans. James Kirkup. New York: New York Review Books, 2001.

———. "James Baldwin: His Voice Remembered; Life in His Language." *New York Times Book Review*, 20 December 1987.

———. *Jazz*. New York: Knopf, 1992.

———. "A Knowing So Deep." *Essence*, May 1985.

———. *Lecture and Speech of Acceptance upon the Award of the Nobel Prize for Literature*. New York: Knopf, 1993.

———. Letter to Obama. http://firstread.msnbc.msn.com/archive/2008/01/28/614795.aspx.

———. *Love*. New York: Knopf, 2003.

———. *A Mercy*. New York: Knopf, 2008.

———. "On the Backs of Blacks." In *The Debate over the Changing Face of America*, edited by Nicolaus Miller, 97–100. New York: Touchstone Books, 1994.

———. "On Behalf of Henry Dumas." *Black American Literature Forum* 22.2 (Summer 1988): 310–12.

———. "On *The Radiance of the King*." *New York Review of Books* 48, no. 13 (2001): 18–20.

———. *Paradise*. New York: Knopf, 1998.

———. *Playing in the Dark: Whiteness and the Literary Imagination*. Cambridge, MA: Harvard University Press, 1992.

———. "Preface to *Deep Sightings and Rescue Missions* by Toni Cade Bambara." In *Deep Sightings and Rescue Missions: Essays, Fiction and Conversations* by Toni Cade Bambara, edited by Erroll McDonald. New York: Pantheon Books, 1996.

———, ed. *Race-ing Justice, En-Gendering Powering: Essays on Anita Hill, Clarence Thomas, and the Construction of Social Reality*. New York: Pantheon, 1992.

———. "The Radiance of the King by Camara Laye." In *Unknown Masterpieces: Writers Rediscover Literature's Hidden Classics*, edited by Edwin Frank. New York: New York Review Books, 2003.

———. "Recitatif." In *Confirmation: An Anthology of African American Women*, edited by Amiri Baraka (LeRoi Jones) and Amina Baraka, 243–61. New York: William Morrow and Company, 1983.

———. "Rediscovering Black History." *New York Times Magazine*, 11 August 1974.

———. "Remarks Given at the Howard University Charter Day Convocation." *Nation* (29 May 1995): 760.

———. *Remember: The Journey to School Integration*. Boston: Houghton, 2004.

———. "Romancing the Shadow." In *The New Romanticism: A Collection of Critical Essays*, edited by Eberhard Alsen, 51–69. New York: Garland, 2000.

———. "Rootedness: The Ancestor as Foundation." In *Black Women Writers (1950–1980): A Critical Evaluation*, edited by Mari Evans, 339–45. Garden City, NY: Anchor, 1984.

———. "Roundtable on the Future of the Humanities in a Fragmented World." *PMLA* 120 (2005): 715–17.

———. "She and Me." In *The Right Words at the Right Time*, edited by Marlo Thomas, 221–23. New York: Simon and Schuster, 2002.

———. "The Site of Memory." In *Inventing the Truth: The Art and Craft of Memoir*, edited by William Zinsser, 103–24. Boston: Houghton, 1987.

———. "A Slow Walk of Trees (as Grandmother Would Say), Hopeless (as Grandfather Would Say)." *New York Times Magazine*, 4 July 1976.

———. *Song of Solomon*. New York, Knopf, 1977.

———. "Speaking of Reynolds Price." In *Critical Essays on Reynolds Price*, edited by James A. Schiff, 44–46. New York: G. K. Hall, 1994.

———. *Sula*. New York: Plume, 1973.

———. "The Talk of the Town." *New Yorker*, 5 October 1998.

———. *Tar Baby*. New York, Knopf, 1981.

———. "To Be a Black Woman." Review of *Portraits in Fact and Fiction*, eds. Mel Watkins and Jay David. *New York Times Book Review*, 23 March 1971.

———. "Toni Morrison on a Book She Loves: Gayl Jones's *Corregidora*." Review of *Corregidora* by Gayl Jones. *Mademoiselle*, May 1975.

———. "Unspeakable Things Unspoken: The Afro-American Presence in American Literature." *Michigan Quarterly Review* 28, no. 1 (1989): 1–34.

———. "What the Black Woman Thinks about Women's Lib." *New York Times Magazine*, 22 August 1971.

———. *What Moves at the Margin: Selected Nonfiction, Toni Morrison*, edited by Carolyn C. Denard. Jackson, MS: University Press of Mississippi, 2008.

Morrison, Toni, and Claudia Brodsky Lacour, eds. *Birth of a Nation'hood: Gaze, Script and Spectacle in the O.J. Simpson Case*. New York: Pantheon, 1997.

Morrison, Toni, and Slade Morrison. *The Big Box*. New York: Hyperion/ Jump at the Sun, 1999.

———. *The Book of Mean People*. New York: Hyperion, 2002.

———. *Who's Got Game? The Ant or the Grasshopper?* New York: Scribner, 2003.

———. *Who's Got Game? The Lion or the Mouse?* New York: Scribner, 2003.

———. *Who's Got Game? The Mirror or the Glass?* New York: Scribner, 2007.

———. *Who's Got Game? The Poppy or the Snake?* New York: Scribner, 2004.

Secondary Print Sources

Als, Hilton. "Ghosts in the House: Profiles." *The New Yorker*, 27 October 2003, 64–75.

Angelo, Bonnie. "The Pain of Being Black." *Time Magazine*, 22 May 1989, 120–122.

Bakerman, Jane, "The Seams Can't Show: An Interview with Toni Morrison." In *Conversations with Toni Morrison*, edited by Danille Taylor-Guthrie, 30. Jackson, MS: University Press of Mississippi, 1994.

Baraka, Amiri. "Introduction." In *Confirmation: An Anthology of African American Women*, edited by Amiri Baraka (LeRoi Jones) and Amina Baraka, 15–26. New York: William Morrow and Company, 1983.

Bearn, Emily. "Toni Morrison: Voice of America's Conscience," *Times Online*, 9 November 2008. http://entertainment.timesonline.co .uk/tol/arts_and_entertainment/books/article5097332.ece.

Beaulieu, Elizabeth Ann, ed. *The Toni Morrison Encyclopedia*. Westport, CT: Greenwood, 2003.

"Bill Clinton the First Black President? Bust a Move, Jokes Barack Obama." NYDailynews.com, 22 January 2008.

Black Creation Annual. "Conversation with Alice Childress and Toni Morrison." In *Conversations with Toni Morrison*, edited by Danille Taylor-Guthrie, 3–9. Jackson, MS: University Press of Mississippi, 1994.

Bloom, Harold, ed. *Toni Morrison*. Philadelphia: Chelsea House Publishers, 2005.

Bouson, J. Brooks. *Quiet as It's Kept: Shame, Trauma, and Race in the Novels of Toni Morrison*. Albany, NY: SUNY Press, 2000.

Brophy-Warren, Jamin. "A Writer's Vote." *The Wall Street Journal*, 7 November 2008.

Carabi, Angels. "Nobel Laureate Toni Morrison Speaks about Her Novel *Jazz*." In *Toni Morrison: Conversations*, edited by Carolyn C. Denard, 91–97. Jackson, MS: University Press of Mississippi, 2008.

"Congressional Black Caucus." CNSNews.com, October 2001.

Conner, Marc C., ed. *The Aesthetics of Toni Morrison: Speaking the Unspeakable*. Jackson, MS: University Press of Mississippi, 2000.

Connolly, Kevin. "Struggle for the African American Vote." *BBC News*, 23 January 2008. http://news.bbc.co.uk/1/hi/world/americas/ 7204182.stm.

Croyden, Margaret. "Toni Morrison Tries Her Hand at Playwriting." In *Conversations with Toni Morrison*, edited by Danille Taylor-Guthrie, 218–22. Jackson, MS: University Press of Mississippi, 1994.

Curry, George. "Bill Clinton: Pimp Daddy President." *The Washington Informer*, 31 January 2008. http://www.washingtoninformer.com/ OPEDGuestCurry 2008Jan31.html.

David, Ron. *Toni Morrison Explained: A Reader's Road Map to the Novels*. New York: Random House, 2000.

Defoe, Daniel. *Robinson Crusoe*. Whitefish, MT: Kessinger Publishing, 2004.

Denard, Carolyn C. "Blacks, Modernism, and the American South: An Interview with Toni Morrison." In *Toni Morrison: Conversations*, edited by Carolyn C. Denard, 178-95. Jackson, MS: University Press of Mississippi, 2008.

———, ed. *Toni Morrison: Conversations*. Jackson, MS: University Press of Mississippi, 2008.

———, ed. *Toni Morrison and the American South*. Special Issue of *Studies in the Literary Imagination* 31, no. 2 (1998): 1–152.

Dowling, Colette. "The Song of Toni Morrison." In *Conversations with Toni Morrison*, edited by Danille Taylor-Guthrie, 48–59. Jackson, MS: University Press of Mississippi, 1994.

Dreifus, Claudia. "Chloe Wofford Talks about Toni Morrison." In *Toni Morrison: Conversations*, edited by Carolyn C. Denard, 98–106. Jackson, MS: University Press of Mississippi, 2008.

Du Bois, W. E. B. *The Souls of Black Folk*. New York: Dover Publications, 1994.

Duvall, John N. *The Identifying Fictions of Toni Morrison: Modernist Authenticity and Postmodern Blackness*. New York: Palgrave, 2000.

Ellison, Ralph. *Shadow and Act*. New York: Vintage International, 1953.

"Faulkner and Women." Faulkner and Yoknapatawpha Conference. In *Toni Morrison: Conversations*, edited by Carolyn C. Denard, 24–28. Jackson, MS: University Press of Mississippi, 2008.

Fultz, Lucille P. *Toni Morrison: Playing with Difference*. Urbana, IL: University of Illinois Press, 2003.

Gates, David. Review of *Paradise* by Toni Morrison. *Newsweek*, 12 January 1998.

Gates, Henry Louis, Jr. *The Signifying Monkey: A Theory of African-American Literary Criticism*. New York: Oxford University Press, 1989.

Gates, Henry Louis, Jr., and K. A. Appiah, eds. *Toni Morrison: Critical Perspectives Past and Present*. New York: Amistad, 1993.

Grewal, Gurleen. *Circles of Sorrow, Lines of Struggle: The Novels of Toni Morrison*. Baton Rouge: Louisiana State University Press, 1998.

Harris, Jessica. "I Will Always Be a Writer." In *Toni Morrison: Conversations*, edited by Carolyn C. Denard, 3–9. Jackson, MS: University Press of Mississippi, 2008.

Haskins, Jim. *Toni Morrison: Telling a Tale Untold*. Brookfield, CT: Twenty-First Century Books, 2003.

Higgins, Therese E. *Religiosity, Cosmology, and Folklore: The African Influence in the Novels of Toni Morrison*. New York: Routledge, 2001.

Hostetler, Ann. "Interview with Toni Morrison: 'The Art of Teaching.'" In *Toni Morrison: Conversations*, edited by Carolyn C. Denard, 196–205. Jackson, MS: University Press of Mississippi, 2008.

Houston, Pam. "Pam Houston Talks with Toni Morrison." In *Toni Morrison: Conversations*, edited by Carolyn C. Denard, 228–59. Jackson, MS: University Press of Mississippi, 2008.

Jaffrey, Zia. "Toni Morrison." In *Toni Morrison: Conversations*, edited by Carolyn C. Denard, 139–54. Jackson, MS: University Press of Mississippi, 2008.

James, Caryn. "Harnessing TV's Power to the Power of the Page." *New York Times*, 21 November 1996.

Jefferson, Margo. "Critic's Notebook; Writing about Race, Walking on Eggshells." *New York Times*, 10 June 1999.

Jones, Bessie W., and Audrey Vinson. "An Interview with Toni Morrison." In *Conversations with Toni Morrison*, edited by Danille Taylor-Guthrie, 171–87. Jackson, MS: University Press of Mississippi, 1994.

Kakutani, Michiko. "Bonds That Seem Cruel Can Be Kind." Review of *A Mercy* by Toni Morrison, *New York Times*, 4 November 2008.

———. "Worthy Women, Unredeemable Men." Review of *Paradise* by Toni Morrison. *New York Times*, 6 January 1998.

Kubitschek, Miss Dehn. *Toni Morrison: A Critical Companion.* Westport, CT: Greenwood, 1998.

Langer, Adam. "Star Power." In *Toni Morrison: Conversations*, edited by Carolyn C. Denard, 206–13. Jackson, MS: University Press of Mississippi, 2008.

LeClair, Thomas. "'The Language Must Not Sweat': A Conversation with Toni Morrison." In *Conversations with Toni Morrison*, edited by Danille Taylor-Guthrie, 119–28. Jackson, MS: University Press of Mississippi, 1994.

Lee, Felicia. "Bench of Memory at Slavery's Gateway." *New York Times*, 28 July 2008.

Lemert, Charles. *Muhammad Ali: Trickster in the Culture of Irony.* New York: Wiley Blackwell, 2003.

Leonard, John. Review of *The Bluest Eye*. *New York Times*, 13 November 1970.

———. "Travels with Toni." *The Nation*, 17 January 1994.

———. "Her Soul's High Song." Review of *Jazz*, by Toni Morrison. *The Nation*, 25 May 1992.

Lester, Rosemarie K. "An Interview with Toni Morrison, Hessian Radio Network, Frankfurt, West Germany." In *Critical Essays on Toni Morrison*, edited by Nellie Y. McKay, 47–54. Boston: G. K. Hall & Co., 1988.

Lorde, Audre. "Uses of the Erotic: The Erotic as Power." In *Sister Outsider: Essays and Speeches by Audre Lorde*, 53–59. Freedom, CA: The Crossing Press, 1984.

Mano, D. Keith. "How to Write Two First Novels with Your Knuckles." *Esquire*, December 1976.

McCluskey, Audrey T. "A Conversation with Toni Morrison." In *Toni Morrison: Conversations*, edited by Carolyn C. Denard, 38–43. Jackson, MS: University Press of Mississippi, 2008.

McKay, Nellie, ed. *Critical Essays on Toni Morrison.* Boston, MA: G. K. Hall, 1988.

———. "An Interview with Toni Morrison." In *Conversations with Toni Morrison*, edited by Danille Taylor-Guthrie, 138–55. Jackson, MS: University Press of Mississippi, 1994.

Middleton, David L., ed. *Toni Morrison's Fiction: Contemporary Criticism*. New York: Garland, 1997.

Morrison, Toni. "A Bench by the Road: Beloved." In *Toni Morrison: Conversations*, edited by Carolyn C. Denard, 44–50. Jackson, MS: University Press of Mississippi, 2008.

———. "Introduction: Friday on the Potomac." In *Race-ing Justice, En-Gendering Powering: Essays on Anita Hill, Clarence Thomas, and the Construction of Social Reality*, edited by Toni Morrison, vii–xxx. New York: Pantheon, 1992.

———. "The Nobel Lecture in Literature." In *What Moves at the Margin: Selected Nonfiction, Toni Morrison*, edited by Carolyn C. Denard, 198–207. Jackson, MS: University Press of Mississippi, 2008.

———. "The Official Story: Dead Man Golfing." In *Birth of a Nation'hood: Gaze, Script and Spectacle in the O.J. Simpson Case*, edited by Toni Morrison and Claudia Brodsky Lacour, vii–xxviii. New York: Pantheon, 1997.

———. "On Behalf of Henry Dumas." In *What Moves at the Margin: Selected Nonfiction, Toni Morrison*, edited by Carolyn C. Denard, 83–85. Jackson, MS: University Press of Mississippi, 2008.

———. "Peril." In *Burn This Book: PEN Writers Speak Out on the Power of the Word*, edited by Toni Morrison, 1–4. New York: HarperStudio, 2009.

———. "Recitatif." In *Before Columbus Foundation Fiction Anthology: Selections from the American Book Awards 1980–1990*, edited by Ishmael Reed, Kathryn Trueblood, and Shawn Wong, 445–64. New York: W. W. Norton, 1992.

———. "Rediscovering Black History." In *What Moves at the Margin: Selected Nonfiction, Toni Morrison*, edited by Carolyn C. Denard, 39–55. Jackson, MS: University Press of Mississippi, 2008.

———. "Rootedness: The Ancestor as Foundation." In *What Moves at the Margin: Selected Nonfiction, Toni Morrison*, edited by Carolyn C. Denard, 56–64. Jackson, MS: University Press of Mississippi, 2008.

———. "She and Me." In *What Moves at the Margin: Selected Nonfiction, Toni Morrison*, edited by Carolyn C. Denard, 15–17. Jackson, MS: University Press of Mississippi, 2008.

———. "A Slow Walk of Trees (as Grandmother Would Say), Hopeless (as Grandfather Would Say)." In *What Moves at the Margin: Selected Nonfiction, Toni Morrison*, edited by Carolyn C. Denard, 3–14. Jackson, MS: University Press of Mississippi, 2008.

———. "The Talk of the Town." In *What Moves at the Margin: Selected Nonfiction, Toni Morrison*, edited by Carolyn C. Denard, 149–53. Jackson, MS: University Press of Mississippi, 2008.

———. "[This Amazing, Troubling Book]." In *Adventures of Huckleberry Finn: An Authoritative Text, Contexts and Source Criticism*, 3rd ed., by Mark Twain, edited by Thomas Cooley, 385–92. New York: W. W. Norton & Company, 1999.

Moyers, Bill. "A Conversation with Toni Morrison." In *Conversations with Toni Morrison*, edited by Danille Taylor-Guthrie, 262–74. Jackson, MS: University Press of Mississippi, 1994.

Naylor, Gloria. "A Conversation: Gloria Naylor and Toni Morrison." In *Conversations with Toni Morrison*, edited by Danille Taylor-Guthrie, 188–217. Jackson, MS: University Press of Mississippi, 1994.

Neal, Larry. "The Black Arts Movement." In *The Portable Sixties Reader*, edited by Ann Charles, 446–53. New York: Penguin Classics, 2003.

"The Nobel Prize in Literature 1993, Toni Morrison." Swedish Academy. October 7, 1993. http://nobelprize.org/nobel_prizes/literature/laureates/1993/press.html.

O'Reilly, Andrea. *Toni Morrison and Motherhood: A Politics of the Heart*. Albany, NY: SUNY Press, 2004.

Otten, Terry. *The Crime of Innocence in the Fiction of Toni Morrison*. Columbia, MO: University of Missouri Press, 1989.

Page, Philip. *Dangerous Freedom: Fusion and Fragmentation in Toni Morrison's Novels*. Jackson, MS: University Press of Mississippi, 1995.

Peach, Linden: *Toni Morrison*. New York: St. Martin's Press, 2000.

Peterson, Nancy J., ed. *Toni Morrison: Critical and Theoretical Approaches*. Baltimore: John Hopkins University Press, 1997.

Peterson, Nancy J., and John Duvall, eds. *Toni Morrison*. Special Issue of *Modern Fiction Studies* 52, no. 2 (2006): 261–541.

Pickert, Kate. "Brief History Oprah's Book Club." *Time*, 26 September 2008.

Ruas, Charles. "Toni Morrison." In *Toni Morrison: Conversations*, edited by Carolyn C. Denard, 93–118. Jackson, MS: University Press of Mississippi, 2008.

Schappell, Elissa. "Toni Morrison: The Art of Fiction." In *Toni Morrison: Conversations*, edited by Carolyn C. Denard, 62–90. Jackson, MS: University Press of Mississippi, 2008.

Smith, Barbara. "Toward a Black Feminist Criticism." In *African American Literary Theory: A Reader*, edited by Winston Napier, 132–46. New York: New York University Press, 2000.

Spillers, Hortense. "A Hateful Passion, A Lost Love: Three Women's Fiction." In *Black, White, and in Color: Essays on American Literature and Culture*, 93–118. Chicago: University of Chicago Press, 2003.

Stepto, Robert. "Intimate Things in Place: A Conversation with Toni Morrison." In *Conversations with Toni Morrison*, edited by Danille Taylor-Guthrie, 10–29. Jackson, MS: University Press of Mississippi, 1994.

Strouse, Jean. "Toni Morrison's Black Magic." *Newsweek*, 30 March 1981.

Tate, Claudia. "Toni Morrison." In *Conversations with Toni Morrison*, edited by Danille Taylor-Guthrie, 156–70. Jackson, MS: University Press of Mississippi, 1994.

Taylor-Guthrie, Danille K., ed. *Conversations with Toni Morrison*. Jackson, MS: University Press of Mississippi, 1994.

"Toni Morrison Finds *A Mercy* in Servitude." Interview by Michele Norris, NPR, 27 October 2008.

"Toni Morrison Talks Obama," *EURWeb.Com*, 7 November 2008. http://www.eurweb.com/story/eur48448.cfm.

Washington, Elsie B. "Talk with Toni Morrison." In *Conversations with Toni Morrison*, edited by Danille Taylor-Guthrie, 234–38. Jackson, MS: University Press of Mississippi, 1994.

Watkins, Mel. "Talk with Toni Morrison." In *Conversations with Toni Morrison*, edited by Danille Taylor-Guthrie, 43–47. Jackson, MS: University Press of Mississippi, 1994.

Nonprint Sources

Anniina's Toni Morrison Page: http://www.luminarium.org/contemporary/tonimorrison/toni.htm

Beloved. VHS, DVD. Directed by Jonathan Demme. Walt Disney Studio, 1999.

Charlie Rose with Toni Morrison. DVD. Charlie Rose, 1998.

Identifiable Qualities: Toni Morrison. Film, VHS. Women Make Movies, 1989.

Nobel Foundation: http://nobelprize.org/nobel_prizes/literature/laureates/1993/morrison-bio.html

Toni Morrison: In Black and White. Film, VHS. Directed by Matteo Bellinelli. RTSI (Switzerland) California Newsreel, 1992.

Toni Morrison: Profile of a Writer. Film, VHS. Homevision, 1987.

The Toni Morrison Society: http://www.tonimorrisonsociety.org/

Toni Morrison: A Writer's Work. Film, VHS. WNET/New York, WTTW/Chicago, and WTVS/Detroit, 2002.

INDEX

ABOUT THE AUTHOR

STEPHANIE LI is an assistant professor of English at the University of Rochester. She received her PhD in English Language and Literature in May 2005 and her MFA in fiction writing in 2003, both from Cornell University. Her research focuses on the ways in which issues of race, class, gender, and sexuality influence conceptions of freedom and determine various modes of resistance. Her forthcoming book, *Something Akin to Freedom: The Choice of Bondage in Narratives by African American Women*, received the First Book Prize in African American Studies from SUNY Press. She is currently guest coediting a special issue of *American Literary History* on the political memoir. She has published in such journals as *Callaloo*, *American Literature*, *Legacy*, and *Studies in American Indian Literatures*.